Praise for *When Grief Calls Forth the Healing*

An arresting and deeply movin[

—*People*

A brave, candid, moving and very well-written memoir of Mary Rockefeller Morgan's life struggle with "twin loss" after the tragic disappearance fifty years ago off the New Guinea coast of her twin brother Michael.

—Peter Matthiessen, two-time winner of the National Book Award

Mary R. Morgan is a gifted psychotherapist, a courageous explorer of the unconscious and a master story teller. She takes us with her as fellow travelers as she discovers the power to heal that is our common birthright as human beings. By sharing her personal journey as well as her experience as a therapist to many others, she helps us trust the natural process of healing which ultimately frees us from grief and carries us safely home. *When Grief Calls Forth the Healing* is an exquisitely written book about the Mystery of twinship. Be prepared for this book to make you less afraid of loss and of life.

—Rachel Naomi Remen, MD, Author of *Kitchen Table Wisdom* and *My Grandfather's Blessings*

When Grief Calls Forth the Healing is a moving, heart-breaking and ultimately gratifying account of one woman's overwhelming loss, struggle and resolution tied to the mysterious disappearance of her twin brother. The loss of a twin has been largely overlooked by the psychological and medical community, but this captivating narrative gives the subject the care and attention it so rightly deserves.

—Dr. Nancy L. Segal, Professor of Developmental Psychology and Director of the Twin Studies Center at California State University, Fullerton, Author, *Someone Else's Twin*

Mary R. Morgan's book is a Gift of the Soul, not only for the twinless twins of the world, but for all of us who search for the answer to the universal question of "Who Am I?" Read it. Admire her and then begin your own search.

In this very moving memoir, Mary R. Morgan shares the deep loss she felt at the disappearance of her twin and the story of her unique healing journey. This book will be equally valuable to lone twins and psychotherapists.

For anyone who has loved another deeply and lost them to death, this book is a boon. For any of us who is a twin and lost their beloved sibling to death, this book is a necessity. With discretion and taste, the reader is taken into Morgan's life story and the hard-won miracle of letting the beloved twin go into his own freedom, and the surviving twin move into the completeness of her own life. This book reaches deep into the psyche and illuminates the soul.

When Grief Calls Forth
the Healing

Mary and Michael, Washington, D.C., 1941

When Grief Calls Forth the Healing

———✦———

A Memoir of Losing a Twin

MARY ROCKEFELLER MORGAN

OPEN ROAD
INTEGRATED MEDIA
NEW YORK

Published in hardcover under the title *Beginning with the End* by Vantage Point Books.

Excerpt from "Little Gidding" from Four Quartets by T.S. Eliot. Copyright © 1942 by T.S. Eliot; Copyright © renewed 1970 by Esme Valerie Eliot. Reprinted by permission of Houghton Mifflin Harcourt Publishing Company. All rights reserved. Grateful acknowledgment is made to the Estate of T.S. Eliot and Faber and Faber Ltd.

Page iv photograph of Mary and Michael Rockefeller by Lena G. Towsley courtesy of Mary R. Morgan.

Page 267 photograph of Michael Rockefeller © President and Fellows of Harvard College, Peabody Museum of Archaeology and Ethnology ID # 2006.15.1.19.30. Photograph by Jan Broekhuijse.

ISBN 978-1-4976-5208-8

This edition published in 2014 by Open Road Integrated Media, Inc.
345 Hudson Street
New York, NY 10014
www.openroadmedia.com

This book is written in loving memory of my twin brother, Michael.

Contents

A FEW WORDS ABOUT THE BOOK

So many people are shattered by deep personal grief, by the unique and often unacknowledged experiences of their loss, and by the misunderstood depth and length of their bereavements. The death of my twin brother, Michael, and the different ways I experienced the absence of him in my life created a deep sense of inner loneliness and outer separation. This memoir recounts that journey of disconnection, and the slow process of putting the pieces of myself back together within the discovery of new connections, and of making a new relationship to both myself and, finally, to my twin brother.

I tell my story in hopes of touching the inconsolably bereaved and of breaking the isolation that surrounds those who have lost a loved one. In sharing the experience of my own twin bereavement, I want to touch the place where other twinless twins are torn from their intrinsic sense of who they are and of how they experience themselves in their lives. I try to shed light on the special challenges they face in their healing journeys.

My own bereavement was unnecessarily long and protracted. Especially as a twin, I found no healing in separation. In making new connections, we break the isolation. Sharing our experiences with others, we form community. Our arms make a circle that can hold the loss, allowing it to be met in safety, allowing for understanding, for listening, for being heard, for being present. In connection, we can bear witness to the necessary process of falling apart and the small steps of coming back together into new form and into new life. By writing and sharing this book, I take my place and invite you into a larger circle of healing connection.

When Grief Calls Forth
the Healing

What we call the beginning is often the end.
And to make an end is to make a beginning.
The end is where we start from.

—T.S. Eliot, "Little Gidding"

MISSING SON OF GOVERNOR ROCKEFELLER DECLARED DEAD

On February 1, 1964, the New York Westchester County Court declared that Michael C. Rockefeller, 23-year-old anthropologist and youngest son of New York Governor Nelson A. Rockefeller, died by drowning on November 19, 1961, off the coast of Dutch New Guinea.

The decision was handed down by Surrogate Court Judge Harry G. Herman. Witness testimony was supported by a Dutch certificate of death, issued April 19, 1962, and by a death certificate issued by the American Foreign Service at Sydney, Australia, June 13, 1962.

Michael Rockefeller disappeared on November 19, 1961, after attempting to swim ashore from a capsized boat off the Asmat coast. The Dutch and Australian navies and local government and populace mounted an exhaustive and ultimately fruitless search along 150 miles of shore and swamp-filled jungle.

Shortly after receiving word of his son's disappearance on November 19, Governor Nelson A. Rockefeller and his daughter Mary, Michael's twin sister, flew to New Guinea to join the search. Rockefeller returned to the United States on November 29, the governor announcing the termination of the mission and that the family was "hoping for a miracle."

Michael C. Rockefeller was born and raised in New York City. He graduated from the Buckley School and Phillips Exeter Academy, and in 1960 from Harvard University with a BA degree in history and economics. After finishing college, he completed basic training at Fort Dix as a member of the U.S. Army Reserves.

In March 1961, Michael joined the Harvard-Peabody Expedition in the Balim Valley, New Guinea, as sound recorder for the film *Dead Birds*. After its completion, he embarked on two trips through the jungles of the Asmat coast to collect Asmat sculpture for the New York Museum of Primitive Art, of which he was a trustee. He lost his life toward the end of his second trip.

In a tribute to his son, Governor Rockefeller said, "Michael had never been happier than in the nine months he spent in New Guinea. He has always loved people and been loved by them. He had tremendous enthusiasm and drive and loved life and beauty in people, in art, and in nature . . . ."

Besides his father, Governor Nelson A. Rockefeller, and twin sister Mary R. Strawbridge, Michael is survived by his mother, Mary C. Rockefeller of New York City; his two brothers, Rodman C. Rockefeller and Steven C. Rockefeller, also of New York City; and his sister Ann R. Pierson of Chicago.[1]

---

[1] This simulated 1964 obituary was compiled by the author from newspaper articles that appeared in *The New York Times*, *New York Daily News*, and *New York Post*, along with added historical information. Due to the circumstances of Michael Rockefeller's disappearance, no formal obituary was ever written.

PART ONE

The Search

CHAPTER ONE

We are in that place of floating again. Tiny arms are holding me. I am holding, too. We are swaying, moved by a gentle breathing sea—new, entwined beings as big as everything, existence held in our arms—the beginning of an "I" held in a frame of "we."

Now I reach that place with my tears. I know my tears belong to the deep. I am drawn to pour them back into the vastness. Darkness folds the roughened water. There are no arms to hold me. My heart will burst with the pain of releasing. I will drown in the empty sea.

THE SEA CHANGE began one day in November 1961. I remember the moment before. A window in the corner of my parents' living room drew my attention. A windblown branch from an azalea bush scratched the surface of the glass, making a discordant sound—an intermittent squeaking. The branch had strayed way past its sculpted boundary. Why hadn't my mother had it pruned?

My father stands out clearly, his figure powerful and solid next to the soft, down-pillowed sofa, his face squared off by his right-angled jaw. By the window, my two brothers and I are clustered around my mother, wary, and watching him. His arrival and bold presence had pushed our little group away and drawn us together. Why had he come? Why had he asked us to meet?

As it was a Sunday, we were gathered at our country home in Pocantico Hills, New York. It was barely two months since Father had separated from our mother. And just days before, he'd called a press conference, choosing to publicly expose his affair and announce his decision to remarry. My brothers and I were still reeling from the family fracture, trying to make sense of our own feelings, trying to support our mother.

Father held a yellow cablegram in his hand. He extended it toward us as if to give reality to his words.

"I have troubling news: This morning, the State Department wired me. I just finished talking to them at Uncle David's. They received word from the Dutch government in New Guinea; they don't know the specifics yet, but Mike is missing."

Missing . . . The 's' sound. Like a thin knife, it slipped deep inside me. No resistance, just a sharp, knowing pain and then shimmering silence. I could feel the shimmering spread, numbing any feeling or sensation. I watched myself retreat from the others.

There must have been questions—anguished, fearful questions. What were my family's reactions? They must have shared some form of horror and then disbelief. I remember the force of Father. He always solved the problem at hand, and he had already come up with a plan. He would go to New Guinea, he said, leaving that night. The family office was arranging for the planes. There he would help to coordinate the search efforts and mobilize the necessary support. And he would charter a small seaplane so he could visit the coastal villages where people knew or had heard of Michael. He wanted to see for himself, to talk to the local villagers. They would know best where Michael might be. Responding to Father's confidence, I found my way back to the group. Within his warmth and within the solid structure of his resolve, I emerged from the silence.

"I want to go with you, Father," I said.

In minutes, everyone agreed it was the right thing for me to do. My older siblings, including Ann in Chicago, had families. Steven was in graduate school, and I was back from the West Coast because my husband, Bill, had recently embarked on a six-month naval cruise in the South Pacific. If I went, Father would not have to go there alone. For me, there was no choice; Michael was my twin.

Yes, I would go with Father to look for Michael. As I joined Father's mission in my mind, lost, engulfed in silence, began to turn into found. And I began to develop my own vision. Father and I would travel together to this foreign land. We would search and we would find Michael. I could even see him when we found him—disheveled, valiant, and even a bit surprised at our concern. Not easily prone to worry or fear, he would have surmounted the obstacles and landed on his feet as he always had. In a fleeting fantasy, I became the princess, departing with my father, the king, to find the lost prince, soon to be reunited in twinship as it was meant to be.

Late that evening, Father and I; Robert Gardner, director of the Harvard Film Study Center and the Harvard-Peabody Expedition to New Guinea; Eliot Elisofon, author and *Life* photographer; Robert McManus, Father's press secretary; and a few other trusted aides boarded a flight to San Francisco and then continued on to Hawaii, where we spent the night.

———

Nap time. We watch bumblebees through the bars of the large wooden crib. The screened-in sun porch, covered in wisteria vines, has become our house. Our time, our house, inside out, outside in.

Hanging purple blooms call droning bees so close we almost touch their sound. Light air lifts your hair and brushes my cheek. It moves with spring's sweet scent.

We're drowsy now, the soft air touching, bees buzzing, flowers sweet. We snuggle closer, curling around each other. Nap time, our time, inside out and outside in.

———

EARLY THE NEXT morning, we started the long journey across the Pacific Ocean to the Dutch East Indies. Finding scheduled flights would have been challenging at best, and focused on the urgency of our mission, Father had chartered a plane to take us, with refueling stops, to the west coast of New Guinea.

We had been accompanied by a few familiar reporters from New York City newspapers on the first leg of the trip, but the news of Michael's disappearance had quickly spread, and in the Honolulu airport we found ourselves surrounded by a growing crowd of journalists. My eyes widened and blinked into a sea of noisy, aggressive faces and flashing lights. Father's somber words, however, satisfied their questions, and their ranks opened and parted, offering us a path to the stairs. I felt his protective arm as we climbed up and away from the reporters into the safe belly of the plane. I never expected that inside we would face a similar scene. We found ourselves within a new group of strange, staring faces, except this time there were no cameras, and the sounds of conversation we heard upon entering turned to expectant silence that spread up and down the aisle as we found our seats in the front of the large cabin.

Father turned and spoke again, welcoming the seated reporters, telling them about the journey ahead, introducing them, revealing his plans for our private now public search for Michael—our Michael, and, I thought fiercely, *my* Michael, not theirs. I felt that these reporters, with their questioning and analyzing—these reporters who seemed to siphon Father's quiet words from his mouth into their notebooks—were stepping on and into our very private lives, into "our mission," as if they were trying to claim it before it could carry itself out on its own.

I didn't dare ask Father why we had to charter such a large plane or why he felt it necessary to play host to this swelling group of press. His arrangements confused, dispirited, and even angered me. As a family, we'd gotten used to the publicity that surrounded us since he'd become governor of New York. I had mixed feelings about the public attention. In the circle of Father's aura, I became an exciting "somebody," but I found this attention fickle and sometimes invasive, and I was becoming aware that any public image I had acquired had little to do with the person I was inside. The fact that I belonged to the Rockefeller family only made the discrepancy worse, for I quickly became the image of people's preconceptions. Now I realized it would be the press corps that would try to define our unfolding reality and create the dominant images.

I must have displaced the anger I felt then at Father onto the press. But I was in way over my head, in a situation without context, holding on for dear life to Father's strength and ability to control our family's destiny and to grasp a victory out of the uncertainty. Sitting beside him, I reached for his hand, for I could feel my own sense of self shrinking, and our fairytale mission beginning to fade and break apart. Where was Michael in this press corps' vision? It was too unsafe to reach for the answer.

"We get out now. See bears!" Michael's eyes gleam in his small, round face.
"Not today," Pat replies, no allowing in her voice. "I've told you, not

until we reach the playground. We're just walking through the zoo."

"Now!" I echo Michael and throw my mittens out of the carriage.

Michael looks at me, then at his mittens. He pulls them off and throws them, too. We giggle and begin to pull at our woolen hats.

"Stop it this minute," exclaims the nurse. She stuffs the fallen mittens back into the carriage. "One more naughty thing and we'll go straight home. You can sit in the dark now and think about what you've done." She unhooks the two accordion hoods from each end of the large, gray pram and closes them together over our heads.

"Geedie?" I whisper our love name in the sudden black dark. "Geedie!" I reach out my hands. No safe shape, no sound, just the feel of a wet mitten. "Where?" I whisper again, frightened. My hand finds a shoe, then a leg. I inch forward.

"Here!" Michael finds the flap of my coat, then my arm. Our hands meet, little fingers curling together—shut tight.

"Bad Pat," Michael whispers, holding on.

"Bad dark," I answer, holding, too.

———

MANY RESTLESS HOURS stretched and stretched out over the endless Pacific Ocean. I hardly slept. I thought of Bill, my husband of eight months, floating somewhere in his troop ship on that huge sea. I wondered if he'd gotten my telegram. No real sense of him came to me—no missing or longing for his touch. This lack of a sense of connection brought with it a vague, fearful shame. I reached back to our wedding day, and then remembered it was the last time I'd seen Mike. Mike and I had danced together, he helping to hold up my long train. We'd laughed about how I'd finally done something first and now it would be his turn. Coming back to the present, I became aware of Father and our "mission." I tried to picture the moment when we would find Michael. But when I got there, I couldn't see him. A vacant space came instead, refusing access to his presence.

———

THE LONG OCEAN flight ended at Wake Island, where we stopped to refuel. From there we flew to Biak, a northern island in the Dutch East Indies. Local dignitaries and Dutch officials waited for us at the base of the metal stairs to the plane. They escorted us through a new and larger throng of flashing lights. Men pointing huge newsreel cameras crowded us to the door of a small anteroom near the waiting area. Inside, we were seated with cold drinks and then given a message to Father from the Dutch government: Michael had "gone missing" from a capsized boat at the entrance to the Eilanden River on the Asmat coast. René Wassing, the Dutch anthropologist and interpreter accompanying Michael, had just been rescued from their partially submerged boat miles from land, but Michael had not been seen since he had left the boat the day before in an attempt to swim ashore.

I have a visual memory of sitting next to Father while he held a press conference for the fifty or more international reporters who clamored for this news. But I have no sense of how I felt about the government report or the words Father spoke. From the newspaper articles I have since read, Father handled himself with dignity as he shared the grim news and extended grateful recognition to all who were organizing the search and helping us get to the Asmat. In one article there was mention of his optimistic outlook and abiding hope.

When the press conference was over, I went in search of a bathroom. It was situated on the outside wall behind the small arrivals building. Alone, I appreciated the privacy but felt trapped in the tiny toilet stall. There seemed no way out; the press had captured Father and me, expanding and moving as we moved. Minutes later, I pushed the bathroom door open upon four or five waiting reporters. I took in their sweating faces: tired, hard, hungry, knowing and encircling me. Their ties were askew, shirts open with sleeves rolled up, jackets flung over arms or shoulders. Their pencils were behind ears or were poised above waiting notebooks, or pushing aside filled pages until a clean sheet appeared.

No fairy tale would spin itself out on those pages. The eyes in those faces—they saw the fear in my heart. I felt surrounded by the very place I did not want to go.

One reporter smiled. "We'd like to know what you think," he said. "How does it feel to have your brother missing at sea—to know that he might have been eaten by a shark?"

"We heard about the headhunting in the Asmat region," another followed. "If your brother made it to shore, do you think the natives might have killed him and taken his head?"

I cannot remember how I got away from them or what I said.

———

"It's time for school; where's Pat?" I follow Michael into Pat's room, dragging my coat. A man's voice comes from the radio:

"I repeat, Franklin Delano Roosevelt, President of the United States, died yesterday afternoon, the twelfth day of April. The family continues to gather at the White House…"

Pat clicks off the news. She sits in her chair, clutching a handkerchief, dabbing at her face. She looks up at us; her eyes are rimmed red. Michael and I step into place next to each other. We look back at her. Pat opens her mouth and closes it again. Tears spill down her cheeks. We have never seen her cry. Her voice begins, hoarse and cracking:

"Yes, school," she says. "Michael, put on your coat. Mary, yours too. And your leggings."

"It's too hot for leggings," I exclaim. "Can't I be like Michael and just wear my coat? Who was that on the radio? Who is dead?"

"Your country's President." Pat hesitates, "And mine, too." Fresh tears spring from her eyes. She covers her face with her hands. Michael pulls on his coat and points at mine. Pat has not noticed it's on the floor. My leggings lie on the bed. I step into these heavy fitted pants, opened at the bottom with zippers. I can't get them over my shoes.

"Please, Pat."

Geedie glowers and pushes me back on the bed. He straightens my legs and struggles with the zippers. I put on my coat.

"I'm sorry, children," Pat murmurs, standing up.

She buttons my coat and the chinstrap hanging from my hat.

We follow her through the hallway and down the stairs in step, our heads bent like hers, our sides touching.

WE LEFT THE big Boeing 707 at Biak and changed to a smaller, two-engine DC-3. The plane took us to Hollandia, the capital of Dutch New Guinea, where we refueled and left immediately for the trip across the mountains to the southeastern Asmat coast. The Owen Stanley Range, with peaks of 17,000 feet, created air drafts that dropped the old plane in precipitous dips. I wasn't frightened; I was too sick.

Jimmy Desmond of the *Daily News* was on the plane, and he wrote in his column of the suffocating, wet heat that filled the cabin of our DC-3 during our descent and remained present from then on throughout our stay in the Asmat. Even though I am very sensitive to temperature, especially to heat, I cannot recall the high temperature and humidity during the Asmat trip, or any of the clothes I wore, or what we had to eat.

When we reached Merauke, a coastal Dutch outpost south of the Asmat territory and the base for the search, a sense of urgency galvanized our immediate group. Father wanted to see where Michael might be found, where his boat had capsized, and the extent of the planned search. We quickly refueled and took off, this time flying low over the coast.

Below our window, as far as my eyes could see, stretched vast jungles, seemingly uninhabited. They were punctuated by meandering rivers, some large, ending in huge spreading deltas. I was struck by the lack of any clear boundary between the land and the ocean. As we dropped closer to the shoreline, we could see row upon row of waves moving in over shallow mud flats, which stretched for a mile or more before meeting the trees. The sun glinted off the water between their trunks, until it was extinguished by the thickening foliage. How could Michael find his way if he made it to shore? This swamp, this huge expanse of trees growing out of water, seemed impossible to navigate.

Where, in all of this, could Michael be? My vision of finding him could not encompass the vast expanse below me or make sense of his disappearance within that watery abyss.

As the plane wove its way back and forth over the 150 miles of desolate coast, I found myself slipping into a fog. Michael and I were lost—but this terrible realization faded even as it materialized, smudged out in a gray fog of inner silence. It was as if I had swallowed an elixir that infused all parts of my body with numb detachment. The fog isolated me from all that surrounded me, even Father. It replaced my vision and Father's mission. It stayed with me through most of the Asmat trip.

CHAPTER TWO

Out the window, the wheels of the big lawn mower roll and clank. I can smell the cut grass. Bluejay calls me. Warm air moves the curtains; it's still hot. My bedside clock reads two o'clock—rest time is over—time for our swim. A while ago I heard the screen door bang; Steven's already gone over to Uncle Laurance's pool. Mike and I meet in the hall in our swimsuits. We've both been waiting—bored, hot, and waiting. We're too old for rests—we're ten.

Uncle Laurance's pool is square and bright blue. On one end there are cement steps; on the other end a diving board. My brother Steven, Michael and I, and our cousins Laura and Marion, are into diving— also swimming under water. We can all dive off the board. We like to dive and pick up the stones we've thrown into the deep end.

Today there's a new game. We're going to dive from the side of the pool and try to swim through the opening under the cement steps. The hole under the pool steps is zigzag in shape. It's easy to bang your head if you don't move into it carefully and at the right angle. Laura and Steven try first, but they give up. They're too big and afraid they'll get stuck. Marion isn't allowed to swim; she's got a cold. That leaves us, Michael and me.

Together we dive from the edge of the pool and glide side by side to the steps to check out the opening. There's something special about us under the water. I haven't asked Geedie, but I think we both feel like fish. Water slides smoothly over our bodies; it's so easy to move, to play, to go on an adventure together. It seems funny we can't breathe down here, funny not to have gills. I hate feeling forced to move up, to move from our world together so we can breathe.

We check out both sides of the opening under the steps; Michael points out the sharp places where the railings are bolted to the cement.

When we climb from the pool, he says he'll go first and I'm to dive after him. In the water again, I imagine we are trout swimming in a stream in and out of the rocks. When Michael disappears into the jagged hole, I follow, wriggling my body to fit through the space. Fish follows fish as we glide out free from the narrow crevice. Michael turns now and grasps my hands. We push off the bottom of the pool. Together we break the surface with a victory shout.

MY MEMORIES FROM our stay in the Asmat are quite discrete and encapsulated. They come from distinct images and feelings, and intuitive-sense reactions, sometimes joined into one recollection and other times separated from each other. It's like the strong image memory I had of the government meeting in the Biak airport, and of Father's subsequent press conference, which both present themselves to me without any feelings or verbal recall. Some events that I participated in and that are clearly described in newspaper reports bring forth no memories at all. The town of Merauke, where we made our base, is one such case. Michael's letters describe Merauke as a remote Dutch coastal outpost with a small airport, available communications, and a large dock where one could hire a boat to travel along the coast to the Asmat region. These facilities were all necessary for the planning and carrying out of the search. No modern amenities were available in the Asmat villages, and only a handful of missionary radio phones existed, scattered over the 10,000 square miles of Asmat jungle.

In his column, Jimmy Desmond described Merauke as a small town with one government hotel where the gathered press—over one hundred journalists—had arrived in separate planes and were put up four to a room. "Other reporters," he wrote, "crammed into a Dutch army barracks; still others scrounged for rooms in private homes."

Father and I had been invited to stay with the Dutch district commissioner and his wife in their small government house. I don't recall meeting or spending time with them, but I know from their letters to Father after we got home that they were hospitable and, in a formal way, kind. I do remember our quarters: a plain, unadorned room with two single beds and an office-like anteroom where Father spent a lot of time on the phone.

In our private time together, there were long moments of silence. I could not reach through my emotional isolation for his warm resolve and strength. We seemed to have emerged into a place where his plan and my vision of finding Michael were like regulation uniforms that no longer fit. For the first time in my life, I noticed lines of worry creasing Father's brow and observed moments when he stared off into space. He drew his comfort from late night calls to Happy, his future wife. I would wake to hear the murmuring of his voice through the door of the anteroom. It created an added barrier between us and brought forth stabs of anger, betrayal, and extreme loneliness that pushed me deeper into the isolation and numbness I had begun to experience on the plane.

———

Breakfast on the terrace is our favorite. Eggs and bacon, pots of jam, heaps of toast. Today, it's late summer; the yellow jackets think they're our guests. Pat hovers around the table waving off the bees.

"Michael, don't touch your toast!" She reaches for his plate, but it's too late. He has already picked up a piece of toast with a yellow jacket perched on its buttery top, its long proboscis deep in a dollop of strawberry jam. We watch together—Michael's fascinated, I'm scared. The yellow jacket's striped hind end raises up and lowers again—up and slowly down as if it's pumping the jam into its mouth. Another bee flies in from the side, landing on Michael's sticky finger. I shriek. He puts down the toast and stares at the new arrival.

Pat, now panicked, cries for him to stop.

"Hold still, Michael. You know it's dangerous. Don't move! I'll get the medicine."

Her fear jumps to my heart and makes me remember: we were very little, Pat said. It happened outside the kitchen door next to Brunhilda's water bowl. Michael put his finger in the water to touch the floating yellow jacket. He got stung, he cried, then he swelled up and couldn't breathe. Mother took him away to the hospital to save his life.

Now I know for sure the bee will sting him. I feel as if I'm going to choke.

"Bees are my friends," Michael says, happily looking up at me. He's smiling, unconcerned with the fear and warnings swirling about his head. A mischievous look comes over his face when Pat rushes back to the table out of breath, clutching the medicine box. He reaches with the first finger of his other hand and very gently strokes the bee once along its back. Then he blows on the side of it, sending it flying off his finger, seemingly undisturbed as it makes its way to the jam pot.

Pat grasps her forehead, which is wet with perspiration. Her shoulders slump with her exhaling breath.

"Don't think your mother won't hear about this, young man," she gasps. She snaps closed the medicine box.

SHORTLY AFTER OUR arrival, a meeting was arranged with René Wassing and the two Dutch officials in charge of the search. Out of this group, only René comes into focus. I can see his slight, small body, his shorts, his ropy muscular legs, his long socks, and his sandals. A dark moustache camouflaged his expression. In the moment before he spoke, I felt fully awake, cleared of the fog within, like a dog on point, listening and sensing, feeling the reality of Michael coming through René's eyes.

René's speech was tinged with nervous anxiety. His English was good enough but difficult at times to understand, masked by his Dutch accent and bad grammar. His nervousness mirrored my own deep anxiety and challenged the place where I clung to hope. I remember René's eyes going from one Dutch official to the other as he spoke. I sensed he felt responsible to them and could not be completely frank with Father and me concerning what had happened to Michael.

My memories of those moments are coming to me mainly through my senses. I have clear images of the meeting but can't be sure of all its content. Over the forty-some years since Michael's disappearance, my recollections and understandings of what happened to him have been augmented, changed, and blurred by various accounts and by sometimes strained and often painful conversations with family, dear friends, and curious acquaintances. Perhaps the facts from Michael's last day were too frightening then for me to fully take in. I also have the feeling I might never have received some of the details, because René might well have been told to keep the story relatively brief in order to spare Father's and my feelings.

The day after our meeting, the reporters, who had gathered in Merauke, had their opportunity to interview René. He gave them a chronological statement of what had happened to him and to Michael before he started to swim, and then answered individual questions. I am quite sure I did not attend that press conference.

At some point after returning home, Bob McManus, Father's press secretary, must have given Father a transcript from a tape of that meeting. I don't believe Father ever shared it with me or anyone else in our family. I discovered the transcript in a sealed file in the family archives, which contain Father's papers, press clippings, letters, and other correspondence related to our trip. Some of the reporters' questions were insensitive and intrusive—even inflammatory. Some of these men, especially those from abroad, sounded like predators, looking and listening for the worst outcome, the possibility of gory details—the meat of a sensational story. However, the transcript is filled with specific and relevant information. I think it comes closest to the truth of what happened to Michael before he left the boat.

Before the start of his second art-collecting trip, Mike had traveled with René from their base in the Asmat village of Agatz to Per, a small coastal village, where he purchased a used Dutch patrol catamaran for their trip. The catamaran was made from two Asmat canoes connected in the middle by a wooden platform; wooden stanchions supported a metal roof. A large, single outboard motor, attached to the platform, powered the boat.

At the beginning of his statement, René explained to the press that he and Michael were joined by two teenage Asmat boys, hired as local dialect translators and general helpers.

They began their last voyage of the second collecting trip on Saturday morning, November 18. The catamaran headed south, along the Asmat coast to the large delta of the Betsj, or Eilanden, River. There they hoped to navigate up this wide river to the smaller river of their destination. In the delta they encountered a rough sea created by the river's outflow mixing with the ocean's incoming tide and strong currents. René said they were not bothered by the choppy water because they had made a similar trip under the same conditions. It was about two p.m. He explained he was at the controls of the outboard motor and had slowed it down when a large wave swamped both canoes, filling them with water and causing the catamaran to sink enough to bring the platform down below the level of the ocean.

Frightened by the swamped boat, the two Asmat boys told René they would try to swim ashore. René and Michael conferred, and then René acquiesced, "It is okay. Just go ahead."

Each boy took a gas can, which they emptied and held on to as they began to swim. René told the press, "We were not at all in a panic in the boat. Michael and I tried to do everything to keep the catamaran floating. We bailed and so on, but it went all so very quickly. A big part of the luggage came loose and floated away toward the ocean."

As the boat sank further into the water, Rene and Michael tried to put what boxes and bags they could save on top of the tin roof. To keep themselves out of the ocean they climbed onto the roof with the luggage, but their top-heavy load made it impossible to keep the craft balanced and the catamaran capsized, throwing them both and most of their cargo into the water. After retrieving some of their baggage, they were able to pull themselves out of the sea and onto the submerged platform. There they sat on the upside-down canoes with their feet resting on the wooden planks in the water. René described how they later pried two boards off the submerged platform to use as paddles, but the strong current and the unwieldy craft made it impossible to navigate or to make any real headway.

In his awkward English, René told the reporters, "We spent the night on top of the raft, for it was more or less a raft now, and we even could sleep a while. We were wet and cold, of course, but we still had our luggage—well, Michael had two wooden boxes and a knapsack, and I had two bags. The rest of our belongings were just gone—all the equipment, all the food, everything." He added that the mostly submerged craft had been drifting steadily out to sea and southward along the coast.

"The next morning it was Sunday. At dawn . . . around half past five, Michael told me, 'Let's try to paddle again to the shore.' It was high tide and so we tried again, but we didn't make much progress. . . . We were much farther away from the coast than the previous day. Then we decided to go ashore, swimming, because it was an accident about the tide. . . . So there was an opportunity, despite the current, to still go to shore. I told Michael I wouldn't dare swim, I'd be exhausted. And he said, 'I think I can make it.' Well, okay, if you make it, I don't do it. I don't take responsibility for you."

René described how Mike pried loose a jerry can stuck underneath one of the canoes. He also had the gasoline tank for the outboard motor, which he had attached to his waist overnight. He loosely bound the two together with his belt so he could lie between them, the cans acting like water wings. He took a Swiss Army knife and a compass with him when he started to swim about seven or eight, the morning of November 19th.

René told the press that the conversation about whether to swim had not been a long one, and again there had been no panic. They had interacted the way they always had during their trips: "calm, cooperative, even with humor." In answer to a question about why Michael decided to swim, René replied that it was "to try and get assistance. . . . At that moment, I didn't know anything about assisting myself or Michael. It was a very small chance to be picked up. Michael said he thought the bigger chance was to go ashore, so there he went. Before he jumped into the water he took off his pants and shoes. I could follow him for quite a while, a half hour or so. I saw him in a straight line going towards shore until I just saw three dots: the two cans and his head."

René answered a reporter's final question by simply saying he could not calculate where Michael might have landed if he had made it to shore. René had mentioned earlier that the land was quite flat and uniform in appearance. It was difficult to tell from that distance how far they had drifted southward and out to sea.

———

IN 1961 THE Asmat was and remains one of the world's most remote and sparsely populated areas. Few boats traveled the coastal area, and only one small seaplane flew along the coast out from and back to Merauke each Friday with the Asmat missionaries' mail. Therefore, in relation to Michael's decision to try to swim ashore, the chances of René and Mike's "raft" being seen or rescued on a Sunday were extremely remote. Also, they could not have survived at sea for any length of time, as their food and water supplies had sunk or floated away with most of their other belongings the previous day when the catamaran capsized.

René was rescued from the floating, overturned catamaran approximately twenty-two hours after Michael left to swim ashore. The two Asmat boys had made it to land across the large river delta after the boat first swamped, and then traveled eleven hours through the watery jungle to the nearest missionary. Neither Mike nor René had thought the Asmat youths would make the extraordinary effort to seek help. The missionary who received the boys radio-phoned for assistance to the Dutch government in Hollandia, which in turn dispatched a navy rescue plane. It air-dropped a rubber life raft with water and supplies to sustain René until a rescue team was able to pick him up by boat the following morning. The rescuers calculated he was about twenty-four miles offshore, and that Michael had been approximately ten or more miles from land when he started to swim.

I go back in my mind to the private meeting Father and I had with the Dutch officials and René at the commissioner's house in Merauke. Images of the grave-faced, bobbing heads of the Dutch officials, the camouflaged expression of René Wassing, and the father I could no longer reach, are all that remain from what might have been stark moments of despair. But then there was the fog. It kept the terrible information I received from reaching my heart, from touching the place from which I could not return.

Michael has "growing pains." That's what Mother calls them. They come mostly in his legs. He is small for his age. I know Mother and Pat are worried he won't grow—I heard them talking about sending him to a doctor. Maybe Geedie's bones are trying hard to stretch and get bigger, and all that stretching is what hurts.

They don't talk to me about it, except to say he will outgrow the pains, but if he's not growing, how is that possible? The worst is when they take him from his room down the hall and put him in the guest room under the stairs next to the dining room. Why do they do that? When it happens, everyone is whispering and I'm not allowed to interrupt or go to him.

I know it hurts a lot because Geedie won't talk about it. If Pat takes him downstairs at night, I wait until I hear her go back to her room. There's a little rug outside the guest room door. I bring my pillow and curl up on it. Sometimes Nacho, our cocker spaniel, lies down next to me. We don't go in to Michael, because I'm afraid I'll get caught. I have to get up quick if I hear Mother walking about above us, for I know she's getting ready to come downstairs. Then I hide in the living room.

When I say my prayers, I pray Michael will grow. I'm taller than him—it doesn't make sense. How can that happen when we're twins?

THE FOLLOWING DAYS were spent waiting for some word about

Michael. Father was preoccupied with plans for the rescue efforts. The Dutch and Australian naval and air units had been sending out helicopters and boats to participate in the search, along with the local Dutch control officers. And many of the Asmat villagers were valiantly combing the small rivers in their canoes for some evidence of Michael.

One morning Father confided that President Kennedy had offered to send a troop transport ship with a contingent of marines to join the search for Michael. However, after weighing all the strategic and political ramifications, and the difficulty of the search terrain, he had declined the President's offer. I accepted his decision without question. Father didn't share with me then that the Dutch government was gravely concerned about the growing threat of an armed conflict with Indonesia, which had been agitating since the end of World War II for the independence of Dutch-held New Guinea (known as West Irian). Years later I was told by an assistant to my father that the Dutch were afraid the search effort would uncover their strategic defenses hidden along the coast. The political environment had to have been tense and complicated, given our presence and the public interest in the search for Michael.

In late 1962 *The New York Times* reported that the Netherlands, through UN negotiation, had agreed to cede West Irian, the last area of their colonial West Indies, to the Indonesians. There was no fight. However, the agreement was not ratified until 1968, six years later.

CHAPTER THREE

I WALKED THROUGH those grim days in the Asmat disconnected from myself, running from the fear of the searchers not finding Michael, running from the fear of what shape he'd be in if they did. Two memorable experiences, however, break through the pervading sense of numbness and isolation and present themselves with great clarity. These memories have stayed with me throughout the years, sometimes bringing tears and always warming my heart.

The first one began on a morning when Father was going through his mail, which arrived by diplomatic pouch every couple of days, courtesy of the Dutch government. He handed me a cablegram, with a surprised smile. It was sent to me by my first cousin Marion, my closest childhood pal. She had taken that year to live in Italy and was studying in Florence. I opened the familiar yellow envelope and found her message. It contained just four words:

Couragio Maria.
Love, Marionna.

Over all those miles, Marion had sent me four connecting words, four words that I could hold on to amid that vast inner and outer sea— four words that felt like a lifeline.

The second memory comes to me from the first trip we took on the Catalina flying boat, the Australian chartered seaplane that carried out the search from the air along the rivers of the Asmat and the many miles of jungle shoreline. News had come to us before we left on that trip that a searcher had picked up a red gasoline can floating near the shore. It was similar to the type of can Mike used as a water wing. Father made plans to comb that area with the plane, stopping at a couple of villages that lined the riverbanks not far from the sea.

We boarded the Catalina from the dock, climbing up transportable metal steps onto the wing of the plane to reach the door of the cockpit. Two large pontoons held the plane's body above the water. When we took off, they slid along the surface of the ocean, sending sheets of spray up against the windows. During our flight Father and I sat together in two of the narrow seats on the coastal side of the plane. I did not focus on who came with us. I moved close to Father, to the comforting smell of his rumpled white shirt with the sleeves rolled up, and stayed next to his solid shape, trying to regain the closeness I used to take for granted.

We landed in the water next to the small village of Amanamkai, which consisted of a row of thatched dwellings raised on stilts lining the muddy riverbank. Trees in dense formation framed the village, and a symphony of squawking, twittering, and flutelike sounds emanated from their branches. Michael had visited this village during his first collecting trip, getting to know the people and making a careful visual and written record of their sculptors' finest work. When we climbed down from the seaplane, which had been pulled next to the dock, the indigenous people who greeted us seemed to have stepped from the pages of Michael's letters.

I tried not to stare, never having seen a community of naked people before. After letting go of my embarrassment, I realized how completely comfortable they were in their bodies. The darkness of their skin allowed me to take in the whole of their shapes. A few of the men wore tattered shorts, and one, an ancient pair of pants. I saw with Michael's eyes how these garments appeared out of place and even seemed to diminish the men's dignity. The climate did not ask for clothes. We were told the Asmat men began to cover themselves after the arrival of the Western missionaries, and now, as Michael had written to Father, "had begun to doubt the worth of their own culture and crave things Western."

A long, narrow, steeply curved, and beautifully carved wooden canoe approached the dock shortly after we arrived. The canoe and the ten men who paddled it appeared as one flowing shape. Water dripped from their paddles in thin sheets, and the sun shone off rolling shoulder muscles, their rhythmic movements merging into a vision of power, pride, and graceful relationship. In a second I understood Mike's excitement and the sense of connection he had described. I recognized a people who lived in harmony with the water and the trees and the sky and the muddy banks of the river. Until then, my Western eyes had taken in this liquid jungle as a forbidden, alien land. But that projection no more fit the moment than the tattered shorts fit the few Asmat men who wore them.

Turning to follow Father and the others in our party leaving the dock, I found myself facing a tiny woman. She stood simply and quietly before me. She allowed me to take in, without hesitation, her naked, old, and wrinkled shape. We looked into each other's eyes. She stretched out her hands to take hold of mine. Silently, she wept.

In the moment of loving kindness that I received from her gaze and her gesture, she offered me a safe passage through my fear and pain surrounding what might have happened or be happening to Michael.

She offered me a way to think of him there, for I had now taken in a reality from his experience. My heart had received the love he must have felt for and from the Asmat people.

Those two experiences became a gift, offering a tiny opening, a hand to hold on to when I was feeling my heart close and the connections break to much of what I understood and loved.

CHAPTER FOUR

Mother announces, "School's out—it's time you two had your own gardens.
No more family victory garden like we had in Washington. You are old
enough to grow your own vegetables. We can eat them at home or maybe if
they are really nice, you can try to sell them to Grandmother and Grandfather
Rockefeller." She stops for a moment and then says, "You should have seen
the vegetables we grew when I was little, and the eggs from our chickens we
would try to sell to Granny and Granpop Clark."

Our eyes widen at the thought of making some money. It's got to be
easier to grow vegetables than it was to dig up onion grass from our hard,
old lawn back in Washington, and I bet we can make more from our
vegetables than five cents for a big bunch of onion grass.

Mother shows us our two small plots next to the large garden where
Augustino, the gardener, tends her roses and where her vegetables are
already growing. She says, "When Augustino comes on Monday, he'll give
you your own tools and show you how to make and measure the rows

with string so you will know where to plant the vegetable seeds."

We go together to the seed store and pick out the ones we want. The seeds come in small paper packets with lovely pictures on the front. I'm growing lettuce, radishes, and carrots, and Michael's growing beans, zucchini, and yellow squash. Michael says his vegetables will be bigger than mine and he will make more money. I say everyone loves carrots and lettuce and maybe they won't like his squash.

Our vegetables are poking up out of the ground! Michael's string beans have long sticks next to them so they can make vines, and I have just thinned out my carrot plants as Augustino showed me.

"Manure." I turn to Michael and stand up. "Remember the cow manure in the big wheelbarrow Augustino spreads over the garden? Our vegetables need food!"

The trowels are locked in the tool shed, so we find some sticks and head over to the field where our two horses and two cows are grazing near the fence. I have borrowed a bucket from the barn and we try to lift the cow manure into it with our sticks. Under its hard crust the manure is gooey and makes me sick. I can tell Michael's getting ready to throw his gross sticks at me, so I run and hide behind the horses. Their poops are nice and dry and round and easy to lift. Back at the garden we dump the manure on the ground. I poke and push and prod the clumps between the rows of lettuce. Michael picks up the manure, crumbles it and spreads it with his hands. He's finished way ahead of me.

"You're such a sissy, Geedie," he grins, standing in the middle of Mother's garden, eating her first tomatoes. I sniff and shake my head. I see the manure on his hands and face and the tomato seeds dribbling through the stains down his chin . . .

It's market day and we head up the big hill to Grandmother and

Grandfather's house with our vegetables in Augustino's wheelbarrow. Michael has two huge zucchinis, three little yellow squashes and a lot of string beans. I have two big bunches of weird-shaped carrots, three little bunches of radishes, and no lettuce—for some reason it did not want to grow. The hill gets steep and we put down the wheelbarrow so we can rest.

"It's true," I say turning to Mike. "Your zucchinis are big and my carrots are full of lumps and sprouts. You have string beans and I don't have any lettuce. I guess you're going to make all the money."

Michael looks at the vegetables and then at me. "It's okay, Geedie," he says, and picks up his side of the wheelbarrow. "It's okay," he smiles. "We'll share." I pick up my side and smile back at him. We start again together, pushing the heavy wheelbarrow up the hill.

WE STAYED IN Merauke for a total of ten days. I know this because I read it in the newspaper accounts. The length of time holds no relevance. How many seaplane journeys did we take along the river and the shoreline? How many meetings did I attend? How many maps did we pore over, and how much waiting time was there without any word? It all blurs together. My fairy tale vision of finding Michael, the wonderful reunion of the king and his daughter with the valiant son-prince—this shimmering myth—had burst in the air like a soap bubble the day we arrived. And the gallant, enthusiastic, problem-solving father had been replaced by an increasingly silent, weighted-down man, his blue-gray eyes barely visible, his strong jaw and mouth etched in grim, downward lines.

At some point Father decided, along with the Dutch government, that the search should end. There was no evidence of Michael or his whereabouts, only the one rusted, red gasoline can.

Rumors and stories of Michael's having made it to shore—of his having been found, captured, and killed by headhunting Asmat villagers—

have persisted for more than forty years. Even today, those conjectures fuel the imagination and help to line the pockets of storytellers, playwrights, filmmakers, and the high-adventure tourist trade. None of them have been substantiated by any concrete evidence. Since 1954 the Dutch government had enforced a ban forbidding tribal warfare and the resulting headhunting that would avenge the death of an important tribal figure. In 1961 we were told that tribal warfare and headhunting had not been eradicated but were rare. All the evidence, based on the strong offshore currents, the high seasonal tides, and the turbulent outgoing waters, as well as the calculations that Michael was approximately ten miles from shore when he began to swim, supports the prevailing theory that he drowned before he was able to reach land.

At the end of our trip, Father made his thank-yous. He gratefully acknowledged the vast and complicated network of support that had contributed to the search for Michael. I was not involved. Looking back, I am aware of how little I helped his efforts. I functioned on the trip as a sheltered, naive, well-mannered twenty-three-year-old, supportive to my father and acting under the auspices of his protection and guidance. It did not occur to me, nor was I given any direction or opportunity, to play another role.

Father made his plans to go home alone. He had requested and received permission from the Secretary of the Navy for my husband, Bill, to be given a week's leave of absence from his ship. I would stay at the U.S. Naval Base at Subic Bay in the Philippines until Bill was able to come and meet me. I left Father in Manila. There I departed for Subic Bay, and Father began his long journey home.

———

"Let's play with our dolls," I say to Michael. "Where are their beds?" Michael pulls them from the toy box under the window in our bedroom,

and I pick up the falling mattresses and the little pillows. We search among the toys for the quilts.

I have a girl doll, and Michael, a boy doll. His has short pants, mine a skirt. The boy's hair is blond, the girl has brown braids. Their hats are the same. Both dolls' clothes are made of green and red plaid. Pat says they are Scotch. We've named them Mary and Michael. We play with the dolls a lot and put them to bed at night.

It's wintertime and our room is cold. Pat has plugged in the space heater. It has coiled springs inside its bars that turn bright red. Nice warm air comes from the heater, and we stay close. Pat has told us never to get near the red coils behind the bars. She is in the next room, knitting in her chair, and we have decided to play "House Fire."

"It's nighttime," says Michael. "The dolls should be in bed. Curtis told me house fires start at night. He read it in the newspaper."

The dolls are under their quilts. I make Mary sit up.

"Michael, wake up," I make her say. "It smells like smoke. Oh, dear, the house is on fire. Michael, Michael! Get up!"

Michael gets his doll out of bed, and we put both dolls against the heater bars with their hands raised up.

"Quick, quick," Michael's doll yells. "We must get out of the house before we burn up." As we pull the dolls back from the heater we see their clothes are smoking and curling up black at the edges.

Pat steps through the doorway into our room. "What!" She turns away. In a minute she is back with a plastic tub full of water from the bathroom and pours it over the dolls' heads.

We are taken to Mother and Father after supper—before bed.

The dolls will never be the same. Their faces are partly melted and their clothes are burned or smudged in black. Their hands are gone—they fell off. Mother says we can't have new dolls because we were very bad. Now we play in Pat's room. Our room is cold all the time. She took away the heater.

CHAPTER FIVE

———————————

I FOUND MYSELF alone within a large sphere and among a series of rectangles—me and my suitcase, me outside any place I had ever known, me without Michael, without Father, feeling no connection to my family or to my new husband whom I was waiting for and who suddenly felt like a stranger.

This sphere was a guesthouse, a Quonset hut on the naval base at Subic Bay, my accommodations for the next week. The one-room building surrounded me like a metal cave, its domed ceiling and sides forming one shape that seemed to sit on a thin wood foundation placed directly on the ground. Its bed, bureau, chair, and night table made up the ill-fitting rectangular shapes. Next to the entrance, a small, square, closetlike room protruded into the space and contained a shower, sink, and toilet. There was no telephone or intercom with service buttons to push, just my watch and the hour I'd been told I would be taken to the admiral's quarters for dinner.

For the first time during the trip I thought of my appearance and my clothes. I lay on the bed, trying to open to this new situation, to cope with the expectations of my hosts, to grasp at an idea of what I might wear. My two dresses were crumpled—neither was clean. My hair was dirty. And worse, rock-bottom dread lurked in this room at the edge of the fog. The outlines of my self folded inward and faded . . .

Suddenly, a high, twittering sound intervened and opened my ears. The sound was close by. It seemed to come from the corrugated metal wall above my head. My eyes focused on a small green lizard about ten inches above the headboard. It clung to the fluted siding with four tiny, protruding, round-toed feet. With its head cocked, it was looking at me and speaking, too. I could feel its high, clear, mesmerizing voice break the vacuum in the closed, round space. The sound found me like the old woman's eyes and held me like her hands. My eyes closed to take in the embrace. When I opened them again, the lizard had begun to climb away, moving over the waves of corrugated tin. It kept up its sweet sound, soothing me, reconnecting me, allowing me to meet the present reality. Somehow it had dared to enter my loneliness and pull me from the fog, choosing to be my little champion in what felt already to be an overwhelming place.

A car, driven by a young ensign, picked me up at seven p.m. Wearing the wrinkled silk suit I'd left home in, I was transported from my geodesic dome to what looked like a white house from an affluent American suburb. It was the South Pacific home of the admiral, the commanding officer of the Subic Bay naval base.

There, twelve people gathered around a long, mahogany dining table for dinner. The men sat in full dress whites with service ribbons lining their chests. Their wives were arranged between them, sheathed in stiff, silk, cowl-necked cocktail dresses. A few wore long evening skirts. The scene reminded me of the seven months of navy life I had just experienced with Bill at the naval base in Coronado, California, right after we were married. As a low-ranking naval officer's wife, I was required to dress up for navy receptions, to wear white gloves, and to put my calling card in a silver bowl on the front hall table when I was invited to the home of a higher-ranking officer.

I was seated next to the admiral, a tall, silver-haired, brusque but seemingly well-meaning man. He leaned in my direction, asking about my father and my family, telling me he had met my uncle John when they both served in the navy during World War II. Feeling distracted and uncomfortable, I tried to answer his questions. Disoriented, I was unable to take in the damask-curtained room lighted by a huge crystal chandelier—this place where silver forks hit china and loud human chatter threatened to obliterate any connection to the swish of paddles and the touch of an old, weathered hand. Everything seemed upside down. These familiar Western sounds felt jarring—alien and isolating. I reached back for the sights and sounds of the Asmat village, for that calming natural scene, the only safe place that could still connect me to Michael.

At a certain point during the meal, the admiral's wife touched her spoon to her wineglass, the crystal sound hushing the garrulous group. She introduced me as "the distinguished Governor Rockefeller's daughter and Michael's twin sister."

Turning from me to the table, she said, "We have all heard about the unfortunate young man who was lost at sea along the New Guinea coast. I don't really know the details, but Mary can fill us in and tell us all about it."

Her round face was cheery and eager. Expectant eyes around the table waited.

"We still have hope they will find my brother," I whispered. Unable to continue, I excused myself and sought refuge in the bathroom.

Water from the tap cooled my burning face. Somehow I found myself back at the table. My conversation with the admiral turned to the job I held for a year after college in New York City. I worked for the New York State Civil Defense Commission, specifically on Father's State Preparedness program, which focused on family protection in case of a nuclear attack. One of my jobs was to give illustrated talks to women's groups throughout the state on how and why to build a fallout shelter.

"Perhaps you would enjoy giving a couple of lectures on building fallout shelters to our staff during the time you spend here," the admiral suggested hopefully. "We could use that kind of information."

My heart sank at the idea. In desperation, I dropped my guard and explained that I honestly did not feel up to it. The admiral's wife had been listening and quickly offered to take me with her the next morning to her weekly bridge game at Clark Air Base.

"We'll fly over there for the day," she explained.

I tried to smile and thank her for her thoughtfulness. After dinner I took her aside to explain that I had no proper or clean clothes to wear and really needed to find a laundry and a store to buy personal supplies. Walking me to the front door, she sighed, "I'll see what I can do, dear."

As we left the admiral's house, everyone expressed excitement about the coming holiday and the USS *Princeton*, the aircraft carrier leaving that evening for the United States, and scheduled to arrive home just in time for Christmas. The admiral took my arm and guided me to his car. I realized that I was to accompany him and his wife to the ceremony for the departing ship.

I feel as if I am in rough water, the guests' happy voices slapping perilously at my head.

We stood on the cement pier, looking up at the arched deck of the *Princeton* towering over us and stretching the length of a football field. The deck was bordered along its top edge by a gleaming white strip, which came into focus as an endless line of sailors' white caps glowing in the twilight sky. The admiral made a short speech. Then, in the following stillness, a thousand male voices began to sing "O Come, All Ye Faithful." Their deep, resonant tones filled the sky. Out of the echoing hush of the carol's ending came an angelic sound—a young tenor singing "O Holy Night." His voice struck my heart like a moonbeam. It pierced the fog, freeing an unbearable longing.

The ensign took me back to the Quonset hut.

———

Michael—desperate wanting and needing him. So much loneliness draws me to the water. I recoil. I won't go there—not to where it leads . . . Above my bed, the tiny lizard . . . I see him silent, bearing witness. Now he calls to my tears, supporting . . . he holds my letting go, guarding . . . he allows my sleep . . .

———

THE NEXT DAY and the days that followed before I left Subic Bay I spent in the company of a young captain's wife whose husband was on sea duty, like mine. I think the admiral's wife finally understood that I would fare better in a family atmosphere with less social pressure and with people closer to my age. The young navy wife took me to shop at the local commissary. I bought toilet articles and some shorts and a bathing suit. In her basement I washed my clothes. I remember sitting with her two sons by the officer's swimming pool. She didn't ask me any questions, just allowed me to stay with her in the moment, watching and helping her with her two little boys as they ran around and splashed in the shallow end of the pool. We ate our meals in her kitchen. I remember how kind she was and how nice the peanut butter looked smeared on her kids' faces.

At the end of the week, Bill arrived at the naval base and we flew to Manila. Father's request had paid off, for Bill had seven days' leave from his ship. I ask myself now how it was for me when I met my new husband after so long a separation. How did I feel when a major piece of my world had disappeared since I had last seen him? We were both so young, so unprepared to grasp or deal with what had happened. Bill was attentive and very sweet. He was optimistic regarding what had happened to Michael.

"I know Mike survived," he stated firmly. "They'll find him, Mary. You'll see."

I really tried, but could not receive the gift of his optimism. The sense of disconnection would not leave. As a result, his kind, well-meaning gestures left me feeling more alone and isolated.

Bill had had his own problems. His troop transport ship was placed on alert when President Kennedy offered to send the marines to search for Michael. Everyone on board had heard about the loss of my brother and soon learned it was their ship that might be diverted to New Guinea. The marines on board were looking forward to going home for Christmas and were understandably upset at the possible change of plans. The crew had also found out that Bill was married to "Michael Rockefeller's twin sister." Bill had had to endure their stares and their barbed jokes, which he even received from some of his own men. He'd lost his anonymity, his ability to grow as an officer in his own right. Overnight he became tagged as one of "those Rockefellers," and a resented and unpopular one at that.

On one level, I felt Bill was as lost as I was. Like two dazed kids, we wandered together through the events of that week. We tried to talk about and plan our life when he got out of the navy. We avoided mentioning my experiences in the Asmat. Bill did not ask, and if he had, I would have been unwilling to share them, not wanting to go there, to try and make sense of something I couldn't understand or begin to deal with myself. We acted like tourists in Manila. After seeing the sights, we ended up at the zoo, where we found an American cow and gaped at a huge and supremely ugly, pink-skinned albino bat.

———

About half an hour before dinner, our family gathers in the living room in New York City to wait for Father to come home. We wait for the low rumble and clank of the elevator door, the jingling of Father's keys, and then the bang of the closing front door. The most exciting thing is the noise of Father's briefcase as he slides it like a bowling ball down the marble tiles of the long vestibule. The briefcase usually ends its journey at the rug under the window opposite the living room. It's that wonderful, swishing, scraping noise that announces that Father is home.

One evening, as Michael and I are playing hopscotch on the black and white marble squares of the vestibule, Father opens the front door, and with a laughing hello, bowls his suitcase into the middle of our game. We jump to get out of its way and continue playing. Father watches us with enthusiasm. We explain that at the beginning and the end of our game, we have to stand with both feet on one black square. Whoever loses balance and falls off loses the game.

"You know, kids," Father says, a sudden seriousness in his eyes, "in real life, you must never get so stuck on one square that you aren't ready to move on to the next one."

I am not sure I understand what Father means, and when I mention it later to Michael, he gets that teasing look.

"I think it's more of a problem for you, Geedie," he says. "I never get stuck on squares."

———

IN THE MIDDLE of the week, Bill and I talked about taking a day trip up into the mountains to a famous whitewater rafting river, which was navigated by Filipino oarsmen in wide-bottomed canoes. We'd been told by some guests at our Manila hotel that if the paddlers made any mistakes during their perilous journey down the tumultuous, boulder-laden stream, the canoes would be dashed upon the rocks. The concierge assured us the trip was safe, that the native oarsmen were seasoned professionals and were required to have years of experience before they were allowed to take tourists down the rapids. We decided to go. The concierge seemed responsible; Bill loved the speed, the water, and the risk, and I felt disconnected from the decision. Perhaps a part of me wanted to follow Michael, to reconnect to him in a ride through the watery oblivion where I felt I had lost him.

It was early afternoon when we arrived at the site. There, the river began with a breathtaking waterfall, dropping a hundred feet into a folded mountain ravine. At its base, the water flowed into a narrow channel that slowed, flattened, and continued smoothly for about one quarter of a mile. An opening on its left bank created space for a small tourist center. We paid for our tickets there and joined the line near the long, thin dock from which the canoes were launched. A dark-skinned, weathered, and bent-over Filipino instructed us to wrap our cameras and wallets in the plastic sheets he handed out and to tie them to our waists. When the waiting line finally disappeared and it was our turn, we were told to sit in the middle of a wide canoe. Two paddlers got in, one at the prow and one in the stern, pushing us off from the dock into the quiet, narrow path of water. On either side, abundant ferns grew from the steep rock walls of the ravine. They quivered and dripped with the spreading mist from the falls. After about three minutes of gliding along its narrow path, the smooth stream began to break into eddies. It quickly lifted into bursts of spray and rapidly undulating currents as we rounded a turn and bore down upon a large group of boulders. Suddenly, our canoe became a swerving roller coaster in deep descent.

The whole ride happened so fast—the rush and the exhilarating feeling of being at one with the canoe and with the wild, surging river. In that moment I experienced without fear the kind of excitement I think Mike found throughout his life.

I could not sustain the brief connection I had made to Michael on the river, despite its being deeply powerful in the moment and now lasting in my memory. Any connection to him inevitably carried me to his disappearance and possible death, which was untenable. I could sense its shadow, a sneaking, bottom-feeding dread. It waited, as before, below the numbing fog and out of sight of the hope that I, and all who cared for Mike, still clung to.

———

AT THE WEEK'S end, Bill left to go back to his ship and I, in a daze, to go home. My KLM flight, a huge prop plane with four engines, carried me with six stops all the way to New York. We departed from Manila for Saigon, Vietnam. From there we flew to Karachi, Pakistan, on to Tehran, Iran, and then to Rome, Italy. Finally, crossing the Atlantic, we stopped to refuel in the Azore Islands. We ended our flight at Idlewild Airport (now John F. Kennedy Airport) in New York.

I am amazed that on the trip home I never once had to change planes. The crew and most of the passengers changed at each stop— a parade of different nationalities, faces, and languages. KLM allowed me to stay in the same seat throughout the long trip. This gave the flight a kind of safe continuity; the plane became a mysterious, homelike space capsule. KLM must have sent word ahead, because the new crews always knew who I was when they arrived and were consistently kind and thoughtful. There were no reporters at any of the airports. Without Father, I was not necessary to their stories. I felt blessed to be left alone.

One time during the two-day trip, the pilots invited me to sit in the cockpit with them while they landed the plane. We were coming into Tehran, and it was dawn when we approached the airport. A glowing pink suffused the huge surrounding desert, turning the approaching mountains to violet. Suddenly, the desert sands lost their pink glow and turned a brilliant white. Behind us, the sun had crossed the horizon. The runway extended like an arrow's path before us. Like the canoe in rushing water, there was a moment of giving over, letting go, and embracing our descent. Thrilling to the moment, I felt the arrow find its mark as we roared down the runway, once again on new ground.

On that plane trip I existed outside the reality of coming home without Michael. The cabin embraced me in encapsulated safety—although I stayed mainly to myself, I was able to watch and listen. The changing language sounds and different facial characteristics of the passengers and the crew fascinated me. Some came from places I had never visited and had only read about in books or seen in the movies.

In Karachi the plane took on an extra engine, which was attached with great fanfare to the wing outside my window. It was to be delivered to the airport in Rome. We were told that weights were being placed on the opposite wing and more fuel added to accommodate the extra load. I was not a courageous flyer. Ordinarily, I would have been glued to the window during the ensuing flight, worried that we didn't have enough power to make our ascent, or that the engine might fall off in flight, tipping us over and causing us to plummet to the ground. Many of the other passengers were anxious. They spoke to me and one another about their concerns, but I felt oddly removed and detached from the potential risk. It was as if I was watching a movie scene outside my window. We took off and arrived in Rome without incident.

Now that we are eight, we often have Sunday lunch at Grandmother and Grandfather's house up on the hill. We go there after church, arriving at a quarter to one. Before the meal, we are allowed to have apple juice or ginger ale. On Sunday, we always eat roast beef and Yorkshire pudding, and Grandmother says we must respect the cook's challenges and be seated at the table at one o'clock.

I love the glass finger bowls lining the sideboard in the dining room. They sit on top of lace doilies that cover the dessert plates. There is about two inches of water in each of the shimmering bowls, with a sweet-smelling geranium leaf floating on top. After the main course is finished, I am given one of the glass bowls. We are supposed to wash our fingers in it and then pick up the bowl, along with its doily, and place it on the top left corner of the table mat so the waitress can serve the dessert.

There is pale green fur on my geranium leaf. I imagine a tiny frog hiding under it about to swim out and jump on its fuzzy leaf top. I stop—I don't want to scare him by touching the water.

"Mary," Grandmother's voice wakes me up. "We're waiting, dear."

Michael giggles. I can feel Mother's disapproving eyes moving back and forth between us. I quickly rinse my hands, churning up the water and overturning the leaf. I tell myself that my little frog has not drowned because he's magic.

After lunch, the grownups always go into the living room for coffee, and Grandfather takes all the children into the library to play Authors or to read Jimmy Brown stories. We don't get to do much with Grandfather by ourselves. This is his special time with us.

Today, it's only Michael and me with him. We're excited and a bit scared. Grandfather's often quiet and he's very strict, but he makes funny little jokes when we are alone with him in the library, and when he reads about Jimmy Brown he seems to love the naughty pranks Jimmy plays on his family.

I am talking with Grandfather about whether to read or play Authors. Michael is over at the desk, playing with a wooden ruler.

"Bring it over to me, Michael," Grandfather says quietly, "and I'll show you how it works." He takes the wooden ruler from Michael. Holding it in a special way, he begins to unfold its sections.

"I often need this ruler," he says, "when I work on my projects. It is excellent for measuring. My father gave it to me—it is very precious."

When the ruler is unfolded, it becomes five feet long, each segment measuring one foot. Grandfather points out the tiny marks of measurement on each side of the ruler—inches on one side, he says, and centimeters on the other. He explains that the ends of the ruler, as well as the joints between each section, are tipped in brass. Michael asks if he can hold it again and Grandfather gives the ruler back to him. I can tell Grandfather is not sure he wants Michael to have it. I'm getting nervous.

"Be careful, Michael. If you want to open it, you must let me guide you."

Geedie is not hearing Grandfather's voice. He is too eager and too quick. SNAP! The wooden ruler breaks in half, leaving two jagged pieces in Michael's hands. The room fills with silence as we stare at the huge mistake.

"Please, Grandfather," I say in a whisper. "I know he didn't mean to do it. We'll find someone to fix it—we will."

Michael's face is all red. He does not want to cry. He keeps trying to fit the pieces together. He's thinking if he wishes hard enough the ruler will mend itself.

"You must learn to listen before you act, Michael." Grandfather's voice is sad and grave. "There are some mistakes you cannot fix."

I don't know who, if anyone, met me at Idlewild Airport at the end of my trip. I do know it wasn't my parents. The early December sky was slate gray and windy in New York, the air exceedingly cold. I felt chilled to the point of shivering. A car took me straight to our family place in Pocantico Hills, to our country home where more than three weeks earlier I had left Mother.

Maybe it was the unexpected, pervasive cold, maybe it was the low crackling sound of the gravel driveway as the car approached our house, maybe it was the top stone of the flagstone steps, its old edges broken and worn, or the small stone sculpture next to the landing of a Mexican family standing in an unbroken circle, their arms holding each other; maybe it was Mother—for as I opened the door I saw her standing there in the front hall waiting for me, and I felt I would fall into a million pieces. Like a child, I ran to her. She hugged me, and I clung in a tearful embrace. Mother's body stiffened. She straightened then and pushed me to arm's length. Her sad brown eyes looked into mine, which were blurred and spilling.

"You must get a hold of yourself, Mary," she said. "The one thing we cannot do now is cry."

PART TWO

The Denial

Darkness!
Pat says, "No light."
I don't know this room, this night,
this longing, this place of not having Mike.

I turn to my side, my knees bend,
One foot curling round the other:
a moment of deep remembering,
of comfort, of things just right.

Now my arms feel empty. They pull the pillow down
from beneath my head.
Black shadows cross the room.
A shapeless form looms in the corner.
Is it moving? Please let it be the chair.
The shape of the window darkens the wall.
Pat pulled down the shade—
Winds are pushing in. The shade grasps the windowsill
and scrapes.

I must look round its edges for the morning.
I am praying for the light.
I pray for our time to get dressed,
to be allowed through Pat's room
to find Geedie, my Mike.

CHAPTER SIX

WHILE I WAITED the six months for Bill to return from his naval deployment, I lived on the East Coast with Mother. During the previous year, I had had my first real job, I had gotten married and left home, my parents had separated, and I had lost my twin brother. Now I was back home again—back to being a dependent, almost to being a child.

My mother had always been a strong role model, and returning from the Asmat I sought refuge in her strength. I trusted, from some central place, that she would rescue me and make sense of the calamity. In denying my tears, she closed the door on that naive assumption. I closed the door on my grief. There was no sanctuary then for my emerging feelings or solace to be found within her embrace.

But from her own perspective, Mother showed the way, and I blindly followed her example, channeling my confusion and despair into the necessary tasks she directed me to carry out. In the ensuing weeks, I helped her find and move into her own place. The terrible pain she must have endured in leaving the home she had made and shared with her husband and her children, and the loss of her husband and youngest son at the same time, were not voiced. Our wounds occupied an unacknowledged space between us. The reality of my own loss diminished. I no longer felt the enveloping fog so present in New Guinea and the Philippines. Instead, my sense of separation expressed itself in my increasing disconnection from my friends, my family, and my life. And the activities of a daily routine drew little inner response from me, as if I had simply stepped out of the world where feelings lived or were engaged.

During the next two months we received no news from the Asmat. Father told me that informal search parties were still going out into the jungle, although they had found no evidence of Michael. Father had arranged for the large collection of Asmat sculpture Michael had procured for the Museum of Primitive Art—over four hundred objects—to be crated and shipped to the United States. Some of these objects—nineteen-foot wooden totem poles and a forty-foot carved wooden canoe—made storage a challenge. They were temporarily housed in the large, empty milking rooms in Grandfather Rockefeller's stone barns. The carvings were painstakingly catalogued from Mike's waterlogged drawings and detailed object notes. His first journal was transcribed; the second had disappeared at sea. The boxes Mike had saved from the water contained these notebooks; René had held on to them on the raft once Mike left to swim, and had given them to Father after he was rescued. I visited the barns to walk through the awesome array of art objects Michael had collected. But everything about Michael was taken in from a distance. Nothing touched my heart.

One day Mother quietly announced it was time to let go of Michael's personal things. I did not question her judgment. We folded Mike's clothes in boxes and set them aside to give away. We put his treasures into the guesthouse living room. These objects and paintings comprised the art he had made or had collected or that had been given to him by Mother and Father, all of which were to be divided among his siblings and his dearest friends. Mother had kept a number of his personal effects—his graduation photos, school yearbooks, the blue Bible Grandmother Rockefeller had given him at our confirmation, as well as many of the personal photographs Michael had taken over the years. She packed them in Mike's now battered and badly discolored suitcase, the one that had arrived home from the Asmat. Was this the one rescued from the sea? I never asked.

In the laundry yard behind the garage, Mother and I piled sticks from the woods and kindling we had found in the fireplace basket in the living room. We placed two cardboard boxes nearby, holding Mike's personal, practical things no one knew what to do with, but which we couldn't bear to throw out. Before gently placing his worn, wooden hairbrush on the pile of wood, I looked to see if there was any hair left in the bristles. Through the inner daze, I knew I wanted it—a little piece of him. There was none. Our housekeeper must have washed the brush in preparation for his homecoming. Mom added to the pile Mike's shaving kit, a pair of old leather slippers with collapsed heels, a cracked and worn baseball glove, and several packs of playing cards. Two half-filled boxes of monogrammed stationery followed, and a peeling leather jewelry box that held tarnished fake-gold cuff links, an old watch strap, and two golf tees.

We burned these pieces of Michael's life, sending up with the smoke the unthinkable, unvoiced message that Michael would not return. We did not cry.

SOMETIME IN THAT winter of 1962 I accompanied Mother to Reno, Nevada. There she lived for two months, at a slightly shabby dude ranch with other soon-to-be divorcées. Mother's stay allowed her to become a legal resident of Nevada, entitling her to file for the quick divorce Father wanted but could not obtain himself if he were to remain governor of New York. He had asked and expected Mother to carry out a divorce she could not accept. She had agreed for the sake of the state and family peace. During our stay, anger at my father burst through my sense of disconnection as if through a special conduit. How could he subject Mother to the indignity of this place? To heck with family peace and the state. Why did Mother agree?

One rainy afternoon we drove into Reno. While Mother went off to do errands, I wandered down a side street into a gambling arcade. I had never witnessed gambling or seen a slot machine. I was fascinated. Small-change machines came first. I put nickels and dimes into each one with no luck. Skipping the quarter machines, I went for the big time. The man in the booth gave me a silver dollar for a paper one, and I placed it into the slot of the showy one-armed bandit. Pulling down its lever, I watched the little windows where the fruits spin. In the left window, three red cherries slowly clicked into place. An immediate grinding noise ensued, followed by the sound of many silver dollars cascading out of the slot machine and on to the floor. I was stunned. I hauled my heavy winnings to church with Mother the following Sunday. The old stone sanctuary stood on Main Street, wedged between the county courthouse and a seedy motel.

"It's all together in Reno for you folks," a cowboy from the ranch had said to me earlier that week with a grin. "You git your divorce, you git remarried, and you git to the motel."

During the offertory at the church service, the usher stopped next to our pew. Judas at Christ's Last Supper flashed into my mind. "Here are your 'thirty pieces of silver,' Father," I whispered and dumped all the heavy coins at once into the offering plate.

I hate Brearley School! I hate learning arithmetic and I can't spell. I hate my sister, Ann, telling me what to do: to button my skirt over my gym bloomers like she thinks she is Pat. I hate Mother and Pat the worst because they made me go to Brearley and have sent Michael to Buckley School with Steven since we came to New York.

Well, I'm home now and I'm going to play with Mike all by myself until dinnertime.

Michael's, Steven's, and Ann's rooms are downstairs in our apartment. I'm on the main floor alone in the room next to Pat down from Roddy's room. He is away at boarding school.

When I open the door to Michael's room it is empty. I hear voices and laughter and head for Steven's room. His room is empty, too, but the noise is coming from his closet.

"Can you see it on yours, Mike?" says Steven. "Can you see Silver's head?"

"Yeah, mine's shining, too—it's really neat."

"What are you doing?" I ask, opening the closet door.

Steven turns. "Get out and close the door," he says.

Mike looks up with an excited face. "We've got the Lone Ranger rings we sent away for," he says. "They shine in the dark. You wanna see?"

"Don't show her, Mike, it's our secret," says Steven, blocking the door. "Anyway, Mary, who said you could come into my room? I didn't give you permission."

Before I know it, Steven's big body and angry voice back me right up and out into the hall. He shuts the door in my face.

Upstairs in my room, I lie down on the bed. There is such a bad feeling in my chest. Now I hate Steven, too, but it doesn't matter. It doesn't seem to do any good.

IN THE LATE spring, Father decided to have a memorial service for Michael. He wrote to each one of us asking for our thoughts, saying that soon it would be six months and, "We need some closure for there is no longer any reasonable chance of finding Michael alive."

We had the service in the Union Church of Pocantico Hills, which stands in the village near our country home. I know about the details of the service because I found the program. I have no memory of that day—of what was done or said during the ceremony. The program lays out a service comprised mainly of prayers. The minister gave a eulogy, but no family member was designated to speak about Michael. It was as if no one could yet bear witness to Michael's life—as if all his loved ones, in their helplessness and vanishing hope, could only take refuge in prayers of solace and the platitudes of a well-meaning minister who hardly knew Michael.

A memorial stone stands amid the ivy ground cover under a tree in our family cemetery; a simple granite headstone. The inscription reads:

In Loving Memory of
Michael Clark Rockefeller
Born New York City
May 18, 1938
Lost at Sea in New Guinea
November 1961

I do not remember our family's making plans about this headstone. Maybe Father made the decision on his own to place it there. We must have had a service in the cemetery, but as with the memorial service, I could not have allowed myself to be present enough to form a memory of these events.

It is Mike's art that allowed me to touch him again during that time. When we were about ten, he had painted a life-size poster of Jesus for the Sunday school. He made it in the shape and style of a stained-glass window. I remember being amazed at how real Jesus looked in the poster and feeling proud when the minister hung it in the vestibule that joins the Sunday school and the church.

In 1956 and 1961, after Grandmother and Grandfather Rockefeller's respective deaths, two memorial stained-glass windows, one created by Matisse and one by Chagall, were installed at the front and back of the Pocantico Hills church. After Michael's memorial service in 1962, Father asked Chagall to come back and design the rest of the windows that lined either side of the nave. One window was to be dedicated to Michael. Chagall heard about Mike's poster and asked to see it before making his design. At the dedication, he told me he was impressed by "young Michael's" artwork. My pride in Michael came rushing back—it was as if he had made the poster yesterday.

———

SOMETIME AFTER THE memorial service, my siblings joined Mother and me at our country house for the division of Michael's things. I chose some very special treasures, paintings that Mike had made and art that had been given to him by Father. I picked things out for Michael's best friends and his girlfriend, Sally. My siblings and I put our choices into separate piles. As I watched and participated in the division of Mike's beloved belongings, feelings welled. His life was being dismembered. We were giving him away. I wasn't ready—I wasn't willing. The family stayed for supper. Making an excuse, I went up to my old room.

The last weeks of my stay with Mother were in her new house in Bedford, New York. There she spent her time answering condolence letters; I was to do the same. Mom had been helpful, giving me printed reply cards for the family to use when answering a stranger's condolence note.

The many personal letters I received had piled up over the previous weeks and lay unopened on the guest room desk. Each day I brought Mother's replies to the mailbox at the end of the driveway and pretended to bring mine. I could not follow her example. I could not carry out this required and important task. I sat at the desk but did not write one letter, not one response to any of the people who felt for me, who had cared enough to reach out and to acknowledge my loss.

CHAPTER SEVEN

BILL CAME BACK to Southern California from his West-Pac cruise in early June. I joined him there for his last year of active duty at the Coronado Naval Base. We again lived in the town of Coronado, this time renting a small, dark, sparsely furnished house on the other side of the large main street. Bill worked at the base from six a.m. until three p.m., with intermittent, brief trips at sea. Most of the time, I stayed home in that colorless plastic space, holding my little black and white mutt on my lap and mindlessly watching daytime television. The TV helped stave off the loneliness. Outside, the Southern California sun drenched the world with blinding light. Within all that brilliance, my sense of isolation grew.

The year before, we had become good friends with one non-navy couple, both doctors. I found momentary relief in their friendship and in their quirky, wonderful kids whom I occasionally babysat. With Bill's encouragement, I tried to make social efforts with his navy friends, but I had never had to learn to cook, clean, or do laundry, and I struggled with household tasks. The challenge of trying to entertain without help was daunting. I pretended I knew what I was doing. Meals with guests consisted of rice, Stouffer's Frozen Lobster Newburg, and Stouffer's Spinach Soufflé.

During this time, my body felt continually ungrounded and off balance, especially outside the house. Bouts of dizziness often forced me to sit or lie down. Our doctor could find no cause for these spells. I was not pregnant, and, as far as he could tell, was in good health.

———

THE FOLLOWING SUMMER, Bill and I moved back to New York City, spending two years in a beautiful apartment belonging to a cousin, which overlooked Central Park. Before we moved in, we stayed for a week in my old home in Pocantico Hills while I packed my things left from my life before my marriage. Throwing out old papers from my desk drawers, I found a brown envelope marked with Michael's name in his handwriting. Inside was a beautiful color photograph he had taken of a screen door with two small lizards on it; one on one side of the screen and one on the other side—two lizards trying to reach each other separated by an impenetrable barrier.

That night I had a dream:

I am tiny; I'm trying to follow the little lizard and his voice up and down the hills and valleys of the Quonset hut's corrugated tin wall. I cannot keep up. The high, twittering voice fades and drowns out in the wind—the waves of tin become the ocean—I cannot swim . . .

The dream woke me, soaked in sweat. I remembered Mother's warning words the day I came home from New Guinea: "We cannot cry." With breath-driven force, I crammed down the fear and the rising, choking tears. And with some hidden resolve, I wrote down the dream. I've kept the photograph and my dream book all these years.

BILL AND I brought our first son, Geoffrey, into the world in the spring of 1964. Motherhood blessed me with the intoxicating, blossoming life of a baby. We were consumed with becoming parents in a community of other young couples with children, and with making our first real home. My depression lifted and the dizziness stopped. I hired a daytime mother's helper and learned how to cook.

Memories of my new life with Bill and my baby son in our apartment overlooking the park are separate from those of the loss of my twin. It's as if I existed in two worlds, one protected from the other. In a few instances, when those worlds intertwined, the memories of Mike still felt isolated, as if held inside an enclosed space.

Newspaper articles from Father's files state that Michael was declared dead by New York's Westchester County Surrogate Court in February 1964. Again, I remember no family announcement or discussion. I felt the impact of the court's decision only when Michael's estate was subsequently settled. A trust of which he was the beneficiary was divided among Michael's siblings according to the number of children each had at the time of his death. I received no money from this trust because I had not had a child by the date of the court's declaration. I was shocked. It wasn't so much the money that upset me; it was the fact that I felt unacknowledged as Michael's twin. No one in my family spoke up or seemed overly concerned when I mentioned the matter. But my twinship felt challenged, even erased. My family's lack of sensitivity further disconnected me from them, deepening the now familiar isolation.

Around the same time that Michael's death was legally affirmed, I began to have strange occurrences of seeing him still alive. I would spot him at the end of a crowded subway car or walking some distance ahead of me down a busy street. On each occasion he would disappear before I could reach him. These experiences came out of the blue and took my breath away. It was all I could do to keep from calling out. One time, when I caught up to a man I thought was Michael, I was stunned to find a stranger. I wrestled with my thoughts, trying to align them with the prevailing wisdom that too much time had passed for him to be alive and not found. But at the same time I secretly nursed the possibility that he *was* alive. Maybe he was living in an extremely remote Asmat village among the artists he loved. Or maybe now he was trying to make his way home. Somehow I would find him or he would just appear. These magical beliefs also existed in an encapsulated place separated most of the time even from myself.

MOVING TO ACCEPT Michael's death, my extended family began to recreate and recognize his life in memory. My brother Rod had given birth to his third son. He wanted to name this child after Michael and telephoned his parents and siblings to be sure we all felt comfortable with his decision. I received his phone call in Austria, where Bill and I had gone for a week's skiing vacation. My first baby wasn't due for several months. Bill and I had thought of naming our child Michael if it was a boy, but I had rejected the idea. It felt wrong. I was not ready. Now Roddy's request shocked and offended me. How could he place my Michael's name on his child? How could I tell him that by his naming his son Michael, my sense of my living twin could be torn from the fabric of myself? I did not express these feelings to Rod. I knew he would find them incomprehensible and certainly unacceptable.

Rod named his third son Michael. Two and a half years later, when my second son was born, I named him Michael. But it was not to express the beauty of my twin's life in the naming of this precious baby. Rather, I made the gesture as a way of desperately holding onto my twin. The split between my reality and the rest of the world's widened.

My sense of separation had become entrenched. I shared my feelings with no one.

———

FOR FAMILY AND friends, finding a way to remember Michael became an important goal. One summer day, six of Mike's closest friends, my sister and brothers and I, and a group of our first cousins all gathered to plan a memorial. In honoring Mike we wanted to bring forth the spirit and quality of his life in a way that would benefit others. We particularly wanted the memorial to be inspired by the purpose and meaning of his travel, study, and adventure among the people of New Guinea.

A quiet joy defines my memory of these exchanges as we reminisced together, appreciating Michael's character, his hopes, and his dreams. I simply did not register that the acceptance of Michael's death underlay the others' motivation for planning the memorial. Again, I was operating within a separate consciousness much as I did when I was on the plane coming back from New Guinea. In my unexpressed, personal mythology, Mike was still away in the Asmat and might return at any time, happily joining us in crafting a plan to further his marvelous discoveries there.

Quite spontaneously the idea emerged for us to form a fellowship at Harvard-Radcliffe, Mike's alma mater. A plan developed: the fellowship would support one or two graduating seniors to spend a year living in a culture other than their own, the way Michael had, enabling them to heighten their sensitivity and awareness, and in so doing, gain a greater understanding of themselves and their world. By removing themselves from the pressures of their own cultural expectations, the recipients would also gain the time and perspective to discover their life's purpose.

All of us were excited and proud of this plan that so beautifully expressed what Michael had done in New Guinea. I was particularly happy because this was our generation's memorial. Since we would not ask for monetary help from our parents, it could only be a small fellowship, but it was our project; we would raise the money among ourselves.

Michael's friends were a special blessing for me. They were a wonderful part of our life as we grew up—almost an extension of our twinship. Now their creative relationship to the fellowship evoked that precious intimacy once again.

Trouble began the next year when the fellowship had been accepted by Harvard, and a board meeting was convened to refine our purpose and select the criteria for the first recipients. Steven and I were voted by our family group to become the first family trustees. A representative from Michael's close friends was also elected. The rest of the members of the board were from Harvard. At about that time, Erik Erikson, the well-known and highly respected developmental psychologist from Harvard, heard about the fellowship. He expressed enthusiasm for our idea of a graduate's spending one year in another culture without pursuing a formal curriculum. It reminded him, he said, of similar pursuits of his own and other young graduates in Germany, a time when German youths could take time out to find themselves before beginning a profession. Dr. Erikson accepted Harvard's invitation to join our initial board of trustees. The whole board was excited by his appointment, for it offered the fellowship immediate credibility and status. Erikson's stories of his own wanderlust, his developmental theories, and his psychological evaluation of Michael's personal journey, delivered in his mesmerizing guttural accent, became a major part of our early meetings. But the development of our founding group's ideas and ideals, so connected to our own personal relationships with Michael, began to feel lost to me, overshadowed by Erikson's professional interests and voice of authority. With dismay, I sensed that Michael's life story was being co-opted and depersonalized—reframed to accord with Erikson's theories.

I understood the value of Erikson's experience and knowledge for the fellowship, and yet I resented his dominating role. My dismay and defensive reactions grew. I felt compelled to become assertive. At one meeting, uneducated opinions and veiled, competitive statements sprang unplanned from my mouth. Erikson took these comments for just so long and then cut me off with a firm, cool rebuke.

"I think it would be appropriate to stop this discussion, Mrs. Strawbridge, and stick with the subject at hand. We have more important decisions to make."

The shame that welled up in me eclipsed my resentment and silenced any positive contribution I might have later made to those early board meetings. I withdrew from the others, disconnecting more deeply from my feelings for and about Michael.

CHAPTER EIGHT

BILL HATED HIS job at the Chemical Bank in New York City. Having grown up in the country outside Philadelphia, he felt confined and depressed by urban life. As a result, after spending three years in New York we moved with our small sons, Geoffrey and Michael, to a house on ten acres of land in the suburbs of White Plains, New York. It was a beautiful home, a stucco and lead-pane-windowed house with low-hanging slate roofs and stone chimneys, which was surrounded by huge tulip trees, a weeping cherry, and on one side, a long stone terrace. Below the terrace, a grassy hill sloped down to a meandering stream. In the distance, across a dirt road, a fenced field bordered a small barn that looked as if it had been carved from the surrounding woods.

Images of the children and our early life in White Plains manifest themselves like a sweet dream: our sons, ages five and three, coming out to greet Bill and me as we lift baby Sabrina from the car in her white wicker basket, gently placing it in their small, eager arms.

"Careful guys, be very careful," I say. "She is so new and so tiny." We slowly walk close together to the front door, Bill and I on either side, guardians of our precious cargo. Sabrina is asleep. Thrilled, the boys concentrate on each step, holding the basket steady.

Now I see fifteen-month-old Sabrina—it's a cold, white-breath day. I pull her up the hill behind our house in our Austrian curled-runner sled. She claps her pudgy knit mittens and laughs at Michael, who has gotten his little skis crossed and topples forward into the snow. Geoffrey is facing down the hill, his skis parallel—no snowplow for him.

"Watch me, Mom, watch me go!"

Tasha, our Newfoundland, barks and follows him down the slope, her long-haired coat rolling back and forth along her spine, her tail up and plumed, black against the snow. Sabrina turns round in the sled and looks at me.

"Cocoa, Mumma, cocoa," she says.

I smile as I call the boys and pull Sabrina up the hill back to the warm house. The pot of cocoa waits for us on the kitchen stove.

Good memories of those years easily emerge. I loved being a mother of little kids, and I loved our big, rambling house. But there was a whole other side of my life in White Plains, which now crowds in.

When Bill and I moved to the country, I brought with me all the expectations of my culture, along with a deep-seated family commitment to community service. During the first year of our life in White Plains, my sense of responsibility was defined by the 1950s. *Mr. Blanding's Dream House* on a larger scale became my dream, as well as becoming the perfect housewife—the perfect wife and the perfect mother. Like my mother, I hired a gardener and a couple to help take care of our home and family. I even employed a secretary, as Mother had, who came once a month to assist me with the bills. Bill and I gave carefully planned dinner parties for our new friends and hosted family get-togethers. I joined a car pool, volunteered at my sons' preschool, and worked part-time at the White Plains Head Start Program.

As the year progressed, the national issues of social injustice in the 1960s pushed more and more into Bill's and my awareness, changing our perspectives. By the next year, I had decided to replace our employment agency couple with a church-recommended Israeli refugee couple accompanied by their fifteen-year-old son. We agreed to sponsor them and do the legal paperwork so they might apply for U.S. residency and obtain green cards. It soon became apparent that this couple had been traumatized by their experiences in German concentration camps as well as by their involvement in two Israeli wars with Palestine. I could not imagine the horror they had suffered. Although they tried hard to help maintain our household, they needed more reassurance and care from me than they were able to give to our home and family. I began to cover for their inadequacies and fix their mistakes. It became increasingly challenging for me to carry out my sense of social responsibility, to care for my family, and at the same time try to run a perfect household.

Bill got a new job as the executive director of the Urban League of Westchester County, an arm of the national civil rights organization. My idea of community service changed to include working on civil rights issues, becoming an activist against commercial nuclear power, and taking a definitive stand against the Vietnam War. In my small and sometimes naive way, I was actively participating in the crumbling of the strict 1950s mores that governed behavior in U.S. cultural and governmental institutions. At the same time I felt confused and sometimes shocked by the mounting social and political changes, and by the conflicting behavior that accompanied them.

One day, an activist friend and I were pushing our toddlers in two strollers on a picket line that wound around a local army recruitment center. As we walked we chanted antiwar slogans. A patrolman who had been monitoring the situation came up behind us, and with an ugly expletive, elbowed past, shoving me in the process into a nearby ditch. Thank God I let go of the stroller. When I caught my breath and climbed out of the dirty trench, my first thought was, "That's outrageous, Sabrina could have been hurt!" Without thinking, I turned to my friend and said, "Let's call a policeman."

Within this charged, conflicted political environment, two of our best friends moved to Canada to protect their teenage sons from the draft. Other friends became polarized, some breaking old social prejudices and boundaries, some clinging to them. I felt the conflict within my family, especially from my oldest brother, who adamantly disrespected my position on the Vietnam War and was only too eager to tell me so. Holding to a progressive stance, I remained a hybrid, trying to balance the social expectations of my post–World War II background with the social responsibilities of a changing world. The roles I was playing became more complicated, were often conflicted, and competed for my time. Life was increasingly hectic. I carried out my tasks with less care and attention to detail. I found myself becoming increasingly critical—both of myself and of others.

Interwoven with the conflicting demands of those years existed the deeply dispiriting, inexorable march that Bill and I were making toward a failed marriage. We had seemed the perfect, socially acceptable 1950s couple. We shared the same background, and our parents were long-time summer friends. We met at the age of four in the baby pool at our local summer club and played together off and on until we began to seriously date during my junior year in college. I broke up with Bill that summer but got back together with him at the end of my senior year. The cultural pressure to marry after college in 1960 and my fear of going off on my own led me to downplay the warning signs of trouble in our early relationship and to accept Bill's proposal. He was handsome and fun, often charming and sweet, and my family approved. Our married life was blessed with important shared social and political values and with shared interests and family expectations. We had three wonderful children together. Despite these advantages, we grew slowly and steadily apart amid serious personal issues.

I was acutely disappointed in myself. I wasn't measuring up. Fear and a deep sense of failure grew, joined by an amorphous dread and the old loneliness. Amid the mounting inner turmoil, my life turned swiftly downward. As if tipped out onto an icy slope, I hurtled out of control to the bottom—to a standstill—to a dead-end afternoon in our garage.

I sit behind the wheel of our station wagon, a lone vehicle in the three-car garage. The space is too big, too empty.

The middle and back seats of the car are filled with the bulging grocery bags from the market. Today is Thursday—the couple's day off. Ethel's here with the kids—she's not working out. Her voice calls from the kitchen—it rises in a high, tinny tone at the end of each phrase. I hate the sound. I'll probably need to help her clean up the toys. She's weird— she doesn't want the boys to take a bath together. Must remind her to fix Sabrina's night bottle. She's been here three weeks and doesn't listen. I know she won't remember Mike's special song—must tell her again about Geoff's cough medicine: I've gotta face it—got to find someone else, a younger person. How will I ever find a good younger person who's fun and knows how to help raise kids?

What's the matter with me? Must get these groceries into the house and put away. Got to see to the kids' dinners and baths and be dressed and back in the car in less than two hours . . . I don't want to but have to . . . have to make the Urban League dinner . . .

If I could just rest—stop the pressure in my head . . .

Oh Lord, I forgot Carol called; she's expecting the money for her parent education program—I haven't raised it . . . can't call anyone tomorrow, have to be at the courthouse for the case to close Indian Point. Why won't people understand the risk? If there's an accident, the prevailing wind will hit Westchester with radiation in the summer and all of New York City in the winter. It's true! Dr. Pollard told Steve . . .

Oh God, Bill's parents are coming this weekend and I haven't invited anyone for dinner . . . must take the boys for a haircut . . . don't want her mean remarks.

I'm so tired . . .

Jesus, I forgot to buy food for the dogs . . .

I watch as my hand moves to turn the car door handle. It can't . . . I'm in a vise. I can't move. Fear—so much fear prickling through my arms—spreading up my chest . . . around my throat . . . too much . . . too much to do . . . I can't get out of the car . . . can't get out . . . can't do it . . . can't do it at all . . . must stop it, stop, stop this terror, stop my life!

There's a little girl now in a single room in a tiny bed, frightened, lonely, a half-child lost in the dark, left behind. I see her . . .

Three small faces look up at me—my children! Their questioning eyes hold mine.

"Oh my God, I am your mother. You are my babies."

The vise breaks. I sit in the car and weep.

———

DRESSED FOR THE Urban League dinner, Bill found me in the garage. I was still sitting in the front seat with the groceries in the back of the car.

CHAPTER NINE

AT THE RECOMMENDATION of my internist, I started seeing a psychiatrist in New York City. My doctor arranged the appointment. I could not seem to make a decision. At home, I went about my tasks in a mechanical way, taking little pleasure from anything I did. I felt removed from everyone except the children—the sole reason for stepping from my bed each morning. The old, familiar fog had returned. Like an automaton, I moved back and forth from our home to the shrink two times a week.

The therapist, Dr. Simmons, welcomed me that first day to his office and began without preamble. He asked background questions in a friendly, direct manner and did not comment on my depressed mood. He did ask at the end of the second session if I felt I could commit a significant amount of time to seeing him. He thought it was important, so I agreed. I sensed he cared and knew what he was doing. The despairing terror that had gripped me in the garage was held at bay by the fog, but the sense of isolation it engendered held angst and foreboding. Dr. Simmons seemed the only way out.

Slowly, over the next several months, I emerged from my depression. Dr. Simmons listened, as I felt ready to talk. He concentrated on my life's tasks and goals, not in terms of my performance, but of what lay behind my expectations. He asked me to begin to differentiate between others' expectations of me and my own values, opinions, and interests. With that perspective and other treatment techniques, he helped me to ease my way out from under my fear and sense of failure. The fog slowly lifted.

The drive to Dr. Simmons's office took about forty minutes. After a few trips, it became part of my healing, a blessed bridge between my sense of disconnection and the listening place I was finding in myself. The station wagon responded in easy, repetitive movements with a steady, purring sound, a mantra blocking out the noise and traffic of the outside world. Within the moving car, I rested in myself. The car erased the road, each light and landmark taking me farther from the "shoulds" and "oughts" I could not fulfill. I looked forward to the trip. The drive into New York offered a space for inner preparation before my session. The drive home became a time for reflection about what I had experienced— a place to catch my breath and find my resolve before reconnecting to the expectations of my life.

After a few weeks, my therapist told me he wanted to give me some psychological tests in order to clarify my therapeutic needs and issues as well as provide added information that would help us plan the goals for my treatment. Using the Rorschach test, Dr. Simmons asked me to describe what various inkblot images reminded me of and what they meant to me.

"All of them look like twins," I said tentatively, sensing the return of the New Guinea fog. "I don't see any separation in these images. I think that's a problem for me."

He did not comment and went on to the next test. But my interpretations of the Rorschach test did bring up for discussion the subject of my twinship and Michael's disappearance in New Guinea. We talked about the Asmat, Father, and the press. I could not get close to what had happened to me. I expressed my outrage about the reporters' behavior as if the experience had happened to someone else. I never mentioned the old woman on the dock and the lizard that became my sustaining friend back in the navy's Quonset hut. I talked about my experience as if it were a terrible movie I had seen. I shared nothing that might touch the pain and call forth the forbidden tears.

Our discussions went in circles. I did not feel safe. Several times, I almost spoke but each time stopped myself on the verge of revealing to Dr. Simmons that I still believed Mike to be alive, and worse, that I felt I might have seen him. After several weeks of holding him at arm's length and during one of our afternoon sessions, Dr. Simmons seemed unusually brusque, certainly less patient with me than he previously had been. He launched into an explanation about twins and genetics, stating that because I was a fraternal and not an identical twin, not to mention a different gender, my genetic relationship to Michael was similar to the one I shared with my other siblings, and therefore my bond to him was no greater than theirs, and neither was my loss.

Finally he looked straight at me and said, "The truth is, Mary, there has been no evidence of your brother's survival in the five years since he disappeared. You need to accept the certainty that Michael is dead. It's time to refocus our work on embracing the full life you have in your own right. It is time now for you to move on."

His clean, cold words closed any opening I had been trying to make in my heart, separating both of us from that fragile inner place.

Dr. Simmons's voice was overpowering. Michael was no closer than any other sibling. Michael was dead. I had to move on. Everyone else in my life had moved on. My friends and family rarely spoke of him, except in terms of the Harvard Fellowship. Mike *must* have died in their minds. I had nowhere to go with my reality. It had to be false. With deep reluctance, I accepted Dr. Simmons's sober logic. It was time to move on.

In our therapy sessions we concentrated on my relationship and reactions to my parents' and to my family's prominence. My father's influence over me and his authority became a huge topic of discussion. Slowly, I was able to connect with my own right to make decisions, develop personal goals, and feel entitled to them, even when they conflicted with others' opinions. It was challenging and important work. I grew stronger inside—not strong enough to question Dr. Simmons's authority or his judgment about the significance of my twinship, but an important part of me "embraced my life," and in that sense, I "moved on."

IN THE FOLLOWING weeks Dr. Simmons and I discussed my growing desire for a space of my own. This desire surfaced in relation to a course in creative writing I was taking at the New School. I wanted to find a quiet place away from home, Bill, and my children—a place where I could be alone and do my writing for the course.

When we explored the issue together, I realized that my desire ran much deeper than the need for privacy to write. I wanted to find a sanctuary within which I could listen to myself. My whole life had been spent defining myself in relation to other people. I had always shared a living space. Now I longed for a place where I could find and define the boundaries of who I was as an individual. Supported by Dr. Simmons, I looked for a small apartment in New York City not far from his office. There I would spend a couple of hours each week in a tiny "home away from home"—private time I would not have to account for.

During the previous few months, I had been reading the feminist writings of Betty Friedan as well as *The Female Eunuch* by Germaine Greer. The emerging feminist movement excited me. I identified with these strong women; their words inspired me to explore my needs and to find the nerve to approach our family lawyer. When I finally made an appointment to see him, I asked him to help me maintain total anonymity while renting an apartment. As I voiced my request, one of his eyebrows slightly raised. I believe he thought I was having an affair. His words and manner, however, remained respectful and professional. He opened an account for me at a separate bank under the name of Mary Greer. In choosing Germaine Greer's name, I felt empowered by an entire social movement. I had a separate identity! As Mary Greer I could free myself of the expectations of what I still experienced as a watching and critical world.

Two weeks later, I walked through the front door of my empty apartment. Giddy with excitement, I claimed my space and my new name. For the first time in my life I felt free.

The little studio apartment became an evolving self-portrait. The paint colors I chose, the furniture I found, the pictures I hung, the tiny kitchen that I equipped with a special cup, a hand-painted plate, an odd silver fork and spoon from a nearby antique shop—all were chosen with a view to expressing who I was in the moment or what I aspired to become. The experience delighted me. I spent hours arranging and rearranging these objects, stepping back to view the results and listening for my reactions. There was no external witness or voice to approve or disapprove of my choices. I listened to music; I listened to the friendly, embracing space. And I began the adventure of creative writing.

The New School professor gave as our first assignment a one-page autobiography that was meant to present the essentials of who we were, "not as someone would describe you from without," he said, "but as you might describe yourself from within."

How could I begin? My mind poured forth a litany of facts describing my life. After listing them on a piece of paper, I realized I was headed in the wrong direction—beginning on the outside, not from within. How would I describe myself from within? Who am I, really?

The clean sheet of paper on my clipboard stares up at me, white and blank. My eyes blur and close . . . I can't sense a critical ear or judging voice . . . I breathe . . . The space inside widens . . . My hand with pencil raised moves to the clipboard and sets off on its own. All of me bears witness as I write:

I am a twin.

CHAPTER TEN

MY TWINSHIP——the very heart of who I experienced myself to be—found no expression beyond the confines of my studio apartment. The one-page biography, which crowned the stack of other completed writing assignments, remained on the dining table, unshared with Dr. Simmons. Those four core words—*I am a twin*—had emerged with stunning clarity from the connection between my mind and my heart, yet I saw no safe place where that connection might lead me. Finding no home in my outer world, these primary words sank back into the unexpressed depths within.

In my therapy and in my life, I continued the struggle to gain a sense of self not defined by others' expectations, needs, and reactions. I developed increasing competency in carrying out the different roles of my life as I learned to set priorities and manage my time. Within the context of that challenging journey, and with deep regret and pain, my eleven-year marriage to Bill ended.

IN THE WET heat of August 1971 I moved with my three children to an apartment in New York City. My parents offered no support during this transition. Instead, my mother expressed deep disapproval. I was the last of her remaining children to terminate a marriage, to let go of what she had held on to despite painful disappointments in her marriage for most of her life. My decision to leave Bill depressed and angered her. She told me I would ruin my children's lives, that I must stay in my marriage for their sake, as she had, and honor my vows despite my problems. Father's life revolved around politics, his new wife, and their two young sons. He was too busy to become involved with my issues, plus his own divorce precluded any judgment of mine.

Mother's disapproving stance hurt, but at the same time, my parents' lack of support and their distance forced me to claim a new independence. For the first time in my life (outside of my little apartment), I made all my decisions on my own. After a few weeks, my sadness over uprooting the children and leaving our beautiful house in Westchester County gave way to excitement about our new home and the potential for our lives in the city where I was born.

In our separation agreement Bill got most of the living room furniture. As a result, I faced an empty living room—a long, rectangular space with three windows at one end. That summer, on a hot afternoon before our move, I sat on the large, dusty floor with a pad and pencil. I surveyed the void surrounding me. It was broken in the middle of the longest wall by an ornate French fireplace, which protruded out into the space bracketed by two large shallow alcoves. An undulating, carved pink marble border framed the opening. The fireplace had no mantel. It was formal, garish, and ugly. I could hear Mother's voice: "It may not be in good taste, Mary, but it's too expensive to replace. Just work around it. You can perfectly well make do." I took in her practical Scottish judgment with familiar irritation, and then felt my father's creative enthusiasm wipe out her voice.

"You know," I said aloud to the space. "If I just got rid of the marble, I could start from the beginning here. I could do it. In this void I can make a new life."

On the paper I drew the room and the fireplace wall as it protruded and indented. I then erased the marble surround, leaving the simple, rectangular opening for the fireplace. From there, I proceeded to design the room based on a repetition of square and rectangular shapes. I chose different shades of gray and tan as my colors, and the soft hues of warm chestnut wood. Brighter colors would come from the artwork. Simple clear shapes grew out of one another. Wall-to-wall carpet covered the floor. The wood base of the constructed sofa platforms connected to and flowed into square box tables covered in the same carpet or made of the warm wood. I used the chestnut wood for a long, narrow shelf. Paralleling the floor, it began at the left side of the protruding fireplace wall and ran above the top of the opening, creating a mantel. The shelf then continued across the wall until it turned the corner and ended deep in the right alcove. There it joined a large, built-in, wooden cabinet, which I drew topped with glass shelves. The left alcove would hold a painting. All the shapes in the room connected and separated the space, creating open space for standing and cozy confined spaces for sitting.

Making the drawing and finding someone to carry out my design gave me the same heady feeling I had experienced in my little studio apartment, with one important difference: I would share this design with the outside world. I was ready; the important thing to me was that I had designed the room myself. The sense of adventure I brought to that endeavor and the pleasure I derived from it made it a success for me.

There was no longer a need for my little apartment, or even the name of Mary Greer. When my lease ran out the next month, I did not renew.

AFTER THE CHILDREN were settled in school, I developed a social life. I felt like a sixteen-year-old when I was asked out on a date. Going out after so many years, going out as a thirty-four-year-old mother of three in a social world that had long since left its strict 1950s mores behind, proved an even more exciting and heady experience than designing my living room. Bill and I were drawn together as teenagers; now I was a mature woman dating mature men. The men I met had varied professions. Some I knew little about. I was curious, soaking up new knowledge and experience within the sophisticated world of big city life.

I also entered a new environment of social expectations. In the permissive 1970s most of the men I met simply assumed I would sleep with them by the second date. Dr. Simmons was interested in my reaction.

"There's no way," I told him. "I'm not ready, and the amazing thing is, I find, without any excuses, I can tell them so."

We laughed together. He was the one person who truly understood how much I had changed.

Tom Morgan entered my life in the spring of 1972. We met at a small dinner party for divorced singles, or so we were labeled on the invitation. Tom made an instant impression. He stood big and tall—an easygoing Midwesterner—enthusiastic, bright, friendly, and definitely attractive. His hair was wavy and dark. He wore glasses and an old sport coat; his bushy, graying mustache outlined a generous smiling mouth. Tom worked in city politics in an exciting and frenetic job as Mayor Lindsay's press secretary. His interest in politics had prompted him to take a temporary leave from his profession as an editor and freelance magazine journalist with a specialty in profile writing.

During that first evening, I observed Tom with interest. I was drawn to the passion and knowledge that he brought to so many facets of political life. When we finally spoke, he made me feel special, soliciting and appreciating my opinions. Our thoughts engaged and spread out, spawning and exploring new ideas. By the end of the evening I was energized; my world had expanded. The respect Tom engendered from those around him and his inclusive attitude toward the whole group added to the attraction.

Within a few weeks of our meeting, Tom and I were seeing each other regularly. After six months, we were seriously committed. We married the following year in a simple ceremony in the apartment I shared with the children. To minimize the change for them, we had decided to make my apartment our home. I set about carving out a special area for us within the large, rambling space. I moved Geoffrey, my oldest son, out of the room next to mine, down the hall into what had been the guest room/playroom, adjacent to my younger son Michael's room. After moving Geoff, I could then create a private space off the main hall that included our bedroom, my study (Geoff's old room), Tom's study/dressing room, and our two baths. A small closet became a kitchenette. Tom was happy with the changes. Although he had two children from a previous marriage, they lived with his ex-wife and were almost grown. At forty-five, he had been on his own for more than ten years.

The domesticity of marriage again drew me in with its work, family routines, and social events. Tom and I shared everything and did everything together in our free time. We even sat next to each other at our square dining table when we hosted dinner parties. Each day I was nourished by the experiences, people, and ideas he brought to our life. At night we were alone, absorbed within the nest of our little home within our home. I loved my children; I felt deeply engaged with and responsible for them, yet I remained unaware of the cocoon of exclusivity I wove around Tom's and my life. I was not sensitive to the effect my obsession with our privacy might have on them as they struggled to accept my marriage, the separation from their father, and the new father figure that had entered their lives.

Tom reached out to my children. He included them within the sphere of his interests, and they shared in his enthusiasm. Through him, they met and enjoyed a whole new range of friends within the world of city politics and journalism. Slowly, with plenty of ups and downs, we began to create a new family.

———

THE VOLUNTEER WORK I undertook in New York City, born out of my sense of family responsibility, gradually reflected my own interests and concerns. I had been appointed to the board of the Metropolitan Museum of Art when I was thirty and still living in White Plains. By the time I moved to New York City, Father, a former trustee, had, after years of negotiation, convinced the museum to accept and exhibit the art of indigenous peoples. In the late 1960s the Met agreed to receive the gift of his collection, which was housed in the Museum of Primitive Art, and to build a wing for it, named in memory of my twin brother. It would feature Michael's collection of Asmat art. Michael had been a board member of Father's small museum for two years before he went to New Guinea. His love of art as a child and young adult, and Father's deep love of art and collecting, had brought the two of them together in a special bond.

Father asked me to join the board of the Museum of Primitive Art in Michael's place. I was honored. When the contract was signed with the Met for his museum to become the Department of the Arts of Africa, Oceania, and the Americas, Father asked me if I, as a board member of both museums, would focus on helping to move the staff and the collection into the Met. He could not shepherd this transition as he was moving to Washington to become the Vice President of the United States under President Gerald Ford. I agreed to become the last president of his museum and to chair the committee of the Met that would coordinate the plans for the transfer of the staff and the design and building of the new wing.

In the months ahead, there were the inevitable philosophical and procedural conflicts between the two museums, as well as interpersonal and political challenges. The Met's director was not a fan of "primitive art"; nor was he interested in collaborative discussions as the way to solve the challenges of merging two museums. And Father, though caught up in Washington with government and White House affairs, did not lose sight of his pet project; thus, I had to chair the committee while navigating between the needs of two institutional staffs and two strong, opinionated men. I had accepted this mandate from Father with pride. Though full of new challenges and often frustrating, this was an exciting and stimulating job. The work I had done with Dr. Simmons allowed me to listen to and learn from others, while beginning to value and trust my own intuition and judgment.

———

WHEN JOHN LINDSAY finished his term as mayor of New York City in 1974, Tom left city politics to become editor of the *Village Voice*, New York's vibrant alternative newspaper. For the next two years, we enjoyed the stimulating world of newspaper journalism. I loved the staff at the *Voice* and the open, irreverent environment of political criticism that they created. Every day held fascinating challenges for Tom, which I enjoyed vicariously. I met many new people in politics, journalism, and business and loved the social life that included them. I hoped Tom would stay on as its editor; however, after Rupert Murdoch bought the *Voice*, he worried about editorial control and decided to step down. The excitement of that experience, as well as Tom's expertise and the pleasure that we found in working together with shared political views and values, led to Tom and me deciding to start our own magazine.

In 1977, with five financial partners and an editorial and administrative staff, we launched *Politicks and Other Human Interests*. This large, newsprint biweekly was created to explore and support citizen participation in the democratic process. We both recognized the power of imagery when combined with the written word, so we designed a magazine that sported full-page social and political drawings. My background as an art history major specializing in graphic art gave me the courage to take on the job of graphics editor. I thrived as part of a large team: talented writers, editors, and artists, working and creating together, depending totally upon one another for the final result—a result I was thrilled to hold in my hands. Every other week we came up with a new issue that we could admire and criticize. We had the opportunity to recreate successes and fix our mistakes. It was wonderfully concrete.

In our work together, Tom and I enjoyed an intimate, easy, familiar connection. He was the boss; he had the knowledge and expertise, but he respected my ability to find and work with artists, and my creative input. I admired the open, easy way he ran the magazine. His office was available to all the staff all the time, except during editorial meetings. However, when he met with me, we would close the door. Everyone knew to leave us alone then. It became a bit of an office joke, but a sweet one.

Politicks and Other Human Interests continued through two years of the Carter administration. We focused on government actions and issues relating to corporate power, equal rights for women, civil rights, gay and lesbian rights, the issues around affirmative action, and the environment. While our subscriptions grew in number, our advertising did not. In 1978 we ran out of money, forcing us to close the magazine at the end of its second year. It was a short, wonderful phase of my life. I felt safely held within my relationship to Tom, and at the same time able to develop my own expertise. Significant also was the fact that my family was not involved in *Politicks*. It was our independent venture. Father, home from his tenure in Washington, made a small effort to admire it, although skeptically and from afar. He never visited our office.

ONE WINTER NIGHT in 1979, my two boys snuck from their beds to watch a forbidden show on television. Suddenly, the program was interrupted by a news bulletin showing their grandfather being carried to an ambulance on a stretcher while the newscaster announced that Vice President Rockefeller had suffered a fatal heart attack. Frightened beyond their fear of reprimand, the boys woke Tom and me.

Father, dead—he had been the backdrop of my life and his huge, engaging personality, power, and influence had created a universe I took for granted. I was stunned. His death threw our entire family upside down and created a vacuum that was hard to fill.

My loss left me confused and shocked—off balance to the point of dizziness. My reaction was physical in that the very shapes of my world distorted. The leaves on trees shimmered out of focus. A new and pervasive dread sent me back into therapy after a five-year hiatus. This time I felt ready for a less directive counselor. My new therapist created a safe, non-judgmental place for me, a place within which I could listen, where I could take the time to wait for the underlying feelings to come—feelings of fear, loss, grief, and anger. Amid that significant transition and loss, I had no conscious thoughts or feelings about Michael. His loss remained hidden from me. Neither my therapist nor I made the connection.

FATHER'S WILL BEQUEATHED the half of his art collection that had been withheld pending the completion of the Rockefeller Wing to the

Metropolitan Museum. As a result, I lost the significant leverage I had had at the Met. Now the museum had no great incentive to carry out Father's wishes regarding any issues or concerns that were not clearly addressed in the contract he had made with the museum and that might potentially conflict with their interests. I had become the only person who could defend his mandate. My task was clear: Besides my own contribution, I must raise the additional monies necessary to complete the wing and fund the design of the art installation. Supported by the loyal staff relationships I had formed and with the collective financial support of family and close friends of Father, I developed the leverage necessary to begin to solve the remaining problems. The greatest challenge was the damaging effect that the sunlight would have as it poured through the glass curtain wall that formed the side of the new south-facing wing. Both Father and the Met had been excited to have the glass curtain wall provide a beautiful view of Central Park that would complement the organic materials of the Oceanic objects exhibited inside. But many of these objects, including two large Easter Island figures as well as Michael's forty-foot Asmat canoe and the six towering *bis* poles, were within range of the bright sunlight from the window.

I joined the Met's Conservation Department in its growing concern for the preservation of these organic materials. However, despite this department's concern, the museum's director was dead set against putting in a protective screen, which he felt would disrupt the view. I thought of Mike and his love for these beautiful and evocative carvings and the extraordinary sculptors who had made them. I remembered his careful efforts to make detailed drawings and descriptions of each sculpture in the collection, grouped under a biography of the artists who had created them. He had plotted and described the artistic styles he discovered, as well as the symbolic images of the carvings of each village and area where they were found. Mike's care and respect for these sculptors' works and for the Asmat people formed the foundation of his realized goal here at the Met.

Anger filled and shielded me. It allowed me to take in that Mike had lost his life in his endeavor to share and give meaning to this art in our Western culture. I vowed I would not let one man's shortsighted agenda destroy Michael's gift. Feeling fiercely protective, I determined to stand for my twin, to save what he had made possible.

After consultation and research, I hired a highly respected conservation expert from a major museum in Europe to assess the situation and make a report. His analysis concluded that the light-exposed collection would be irrevocably damaged within three years. I called each of the donors to explain the findings and asked them to sign a statement making our financial gift contingent on the screening of the window according to the specifications of the report. They agreed. The Met, after brief consultation, gave in.

Six months later, as the installation date for the collection neared, the screen had not been installed. The director told me the museum could not find a screen as dense as required in the expert's report and had decided to order a lighter one. When I questioned this solution, he patted me on the top of my head.

"Don't worry your pretty head about it, Mary," he said. "Just go off to East Hampton or wherever you go for your vacation. The screen will be fine."

"I'm afraid it won't," I answered, "unless it's the prescribed density. I don't think you understand how clear our donors' letter is on that point, and we will stick to it."

He knew I meant it. The screen with its prescribed density was in place before the collection was installed. Now the view of Central Park shows through the gray screen mesh in shadowy outline, as if the arching trees appear through a mist. The effect is mysterious and quite beautiful.

The wing opened in 1982, three years after Father's death. On that day, as with the launch of the Rockefeller Fellowship, feelings of joy and pride in my twin brother flowed without interruption. Michael's love of Asmat art and his growing appreciation for the primary role it played within the cultural, spiritual, and everyday lives of the coastal people who carved it had resulted in a collection that enhanced the museum. For me, it crowned the wing's collection. In the opening ceremony, as I paid respect to the dignitaries from the countries and cultures represented in the wing, I experienced Michael's life transmuted into a perpetuating gift. For one beautiful day I was lifted from the dark shadow of loss.

My cousin Marion and I are in trouble. Last night, we snuck out of our houses at 11 p.m. and met at the barn for our night ride. We got caught, but it's even worse than that.

We've been getting ourselves ready for our midnight ride to try and see the Headless Horseman who gallops down the Sleepy Hollow road when the moon is full. We are going alone, not even with Mike. We're practicing riding at night so we can get used to seeing in the dark and the horses won't get spooked.

Yesterday, we decided to practice on the golf course where there aren't so many trees. Actually, it's a lot of fun because we can gallop really fast—good in case the Headless Horseman comes after us. We've decided to be Indians so we aren't using saddles or bridles, just a rope around Prince and Queenie's noses. This way, we can flatten our bodies along their backs and move even faster. We'd been practicing stopping and starting and turning. The problem is we didn't notice the soft places on the lawn where you start and stop the golf game.

This morning after breakfast, Aunt Mary called Mom to say that Grandfather had telephoned to tell her that two people had ridden horseback all over the golf course and had torn up two or three of the golf greens. Marion has already confessed. They probably made her tell. Mother is furious! We had to go up to see Grandfather after lunch in his study. I'm in my room now where Mom told me to stay until dinner and think about what he said.

Up at the Big House, Marion and I were really scared. Grandfather was quiet. He looked very angry. What we did was thoughtless, he said. And what we did showed no concern for others, and no responsibility for the gift of our family place. To make up for our disrespect, he told us we needed to contribute to the welfare of the estate. Our punishment is to paint the two workrooms in the guard dog kennels. Grandfather told us we couldn't ask for help; we must figure out how to do the job ourselves. We have to work every day in the kennels until it's done. We even have to give up our afternoon swimming. Also, Mother and Aunt Mary told us we couldn't ride for two weeks. The horses have been turned out in the field between our houses. Worse, when we ride again this summer, we aren't allowed out on the trails without someone with us.

Well, it has been over a week and we're still not out of trouble. We bought gallons of brown and peach paint on Mother's account at the hardware store. We've spent the whole week painting the two rooms where the dogs are bathed and fed. The problem is the windows. We agreed to paint everything brown except for the large borders around the windows and the wood that surrounds the small window panes and the window-sills. We are painting those peach. We should have let the paint dry before we changed color. Now the brown has run down into the peach and onto the glass windows. It's a mess. Geedie, where are you?

Yesterday morning, we snuck Mike into the kennels. He was playing with Steven. I'm praying Steven won't tell. Michael loves the dogs so when he came in they didn't even bark. So far, no one's found out.

When Geedie saw our work, he just stood still in the middle of the room.

"Peach," he said, looking at the ceiling and the windows. "What kind of color is that for a dog kennel?"

"We like it," Marion and I said almost in unison. "Anyway, we didn't ask your opinion—just your help."

Mike started grinning and shaking his head. I know he was picturing Grandfather's reaction. Well, so what—we didn't have enough paint to change anything. And it was so hot all we could think about was swimming.

"Let the windows dry another day," Geedie told us. He then helped us finish painting the ceiling. The next day, he got a scraper and some small brushes from the painter who was redoing Uncle Laurance's kitchen. For the next three mornings, we scraped off the peach paint where it had run onto the windows and repainted the wood between the panes of glass, and then the windowsills. Mike is so careful. He knew just what to tell us, and just what to do.

"Where did you learn?" I asked him.

"I don't know, I like paint," he said. "I just watch."

After ten days, we are done and Grandfather has come to inspect. Marion and I apologize again and say we will always respect our family place. I know Grandfather is pleased. He smiles and doesn't say anything about the peach—I don't think that would have happened without Geedie. We tell him our secret about the Headless Horseman. It doesn't seem so important to find him anymore. Geedie says tomorrow is August. He's talking about sailing—we're going to Maine.

CHAPTER ELEVEN

A TREASURED FRIENDSHIP lay within my healing journey. It began in 1974 and wove its way like a golden thread through the years until it ended soon after the Rockefeller Wing opened in 1982.

When Tom was named editor of the *Village Voice*, he hired as his assistant a young woman named Mary Margaret Goodrich. M.M., as everyone called her, soon became an indispensable part of the work and life of the *Voice*, and her presence created an infectiously delightful atmosphere. I loved her from the first day I met her. One winter afternoon, the children and I were invited to make our introductory visit to the newspaper, and Tom, up against a deadline, asked M.M. to introduce us to what he had described as "the wild, creative, and thoroughly original world of the *Voice*."

I remember looking for Tom's office on the crowded second floor. The three children and I wound our way through the clutter of tables and desks, the clatter of typewriters, and the curious glances of the newspaper staff. Near Tom's door we came upon a small person, her face almost obscured by the pile of papers she held in her arms.

"You must be Tom's wife and kids," she said, dumping the papers unceremoniously on her desk. Her face broke into a radiant grin. "I'm M.M., Tom's assistant. Welcome to our zoo. Welcome to the *Voice*."

"Where are the animals?" four-year-old Sabrina asked.

"Well," M.M. answered, helping Sabrina off with her coat, "there's one behind every desk, and two at the managing editor's desk—you'll see."

"She's teasing you, Dodo," Geoffrey whispered.

M.M. giggled, and before I knew it, she had all three kids photographing their hands in the Xerox machine and happily playing with the managing editor's dog, which hung out under her big desk. M.M. introduced me to the staff, from editors to copy boys. We felt thoroughly welcomed; actually, as I told Tom later, we felt at home.

Whenever I would call Tom at the *Voice*, M.M. answered his phone. She always managed to say something that lightened my heart and made me smile. She poked fun at the pompous, laughed at herself, and was never mean-spirited. Most everyone at the magazine loved her. If they weren't charmed and drawn to her playful, earthy wit, they were warmed by her inclusiveness.

A little over a year after Tom started as editor, Mary Margaret became ill and left the *Voice*. She had developed chronic endometriosis, which evolved into endometrial cancer. She sought treatment in New York City, but her illness soon prevented her from continuing to work, and she decided to return home to Brownsville, Texas to be near her parents.

Rather than ending, our relationship deepened. What had begun as brief, humorous chats whenever I called Tom, and delightful conversations at *Village Voice* functions, now turned into regular long-distance phone calls. M.M.'s warm, generous heart and unique spirit drew me to her. Through our lengthy conversations I discovered a courageous and interesting woman, deeply committed to growing from her experiences.

After surgery and chemotherapy at the MD Anderson Cancer Center in Texas, M.M. went into remission and moved to Boulder, Colorado. She came back to New York City to visit and stayed for a few weekends at our country house. Despite her illness, she continued to delight those around her. All my mischievous instincts awakened in her presence. I dropped any self-editing and felt gloriously able to play. We laughed constantly. Following her lead, I even started to make fun of myself.

With a feeling of curious familiarity, I noticed that M.M. and I spontaneously trusted each other, a trust that grew as we shared our personal vulnerabilities and failures without fear of diminishing our mutual regard. I adored the practical, direct way she dealt with her world and its challenges, and her willingness to confront her own as well as my unspoken fears.

After her first round of difficult treatments and painful surgery, it became necessary to remove her colon, and M.M. had to resort to wearing a colostomy bag. One morning, during a visit I made to be with her in Boulder, we were standing in her bathroom preparing to take turns in the shower. Out of the blue she announced to me that it was about time I dropped my fear of her operation—*how did she know?*—and my horror at her having to cope with using "those little shit bags," as she called the plastic colostomy bags that she now pulled out from under the sink.

"Come on, Mary," she said with a twinkle. "You'll see."

Without giving me time to react, she dropped her towel to the floor and pointed to a small opening on the lower left side of her waist. It looked like a tiny, closed mouth—like nature had fashioned it there by mistake. She showed me how the colostomy bag fit snuggly over this opening, and how easy it was to remove and dispose of.

"See what I mean, Mare?" she finished, stepping into the shower with a broad grin. "It's really no big deal."

It *was* no big deal. She'd seen to it—my fear had vanished.

DURING MY VISIT with Mary Margaret in Boulder, we spent a day up in the mountains. We wore rain pants over our ski pants and did yoga in the snow. M.M. had lost her hair from the chemotherapy. Her head was wrapped in a colorful scarf. She glowed in the sunlight, like some enchanted genie sitting cross-legged on her white carpet. Her health had begun to fail again, yet her spirit was radiant.

Down from the mountain we went for tea in a local Boulder café. From her pocket, M.M. pulled out a small, blank-paged book covered in a muted flower-and-leaf-patterned velvet. A narrow grosgrain ribbon hung down from its spine to mark the pages. As she handed it to me, she explained that this was a work in progress that would become her gift to me. I opened the front page to an inscription, which read: "A book for my magnificent Mary Morgan from Mary Margaret, May 15th, 1981."

On the next page she had made a delicate pen and wash drawing of three old bottles that we had found together in a secondhand shop. Facing that page was a letter:

> Dear Mary, . . . I made a revolutionary decision at the end
> of last month: to cease looking for any outer authority
> and instead be guided by Me within, so *heureusement* or
> *malheureusement* this book will be expressions of my own
> religion set down with Massive love for you who have given
> such Massive love to me, with of course, the ever-underlying
> terror that, now that I have no other outer authority, WHAT
> IF GOD DOESN'T TALK TO US?

Over the next year, M.M. filled her little book with the daily challenges of her illness; her struggles to understand the meaning of her existence; her physical pain, yearnings, and awakenings; and the continued joy she found in living every day fully. Her entries are interspersed with her colorful and original drawings. In the years of our friendship, M.M. had begun to share her spiritual beliefs with me and had increased her inquiry into the personal meaning of divinity. She came to the realization that she was part of and belonged to a divine greater whole—which she defined as God. I watched her spiritual connection grow until it became a part of the fabric of her life. And, as with everything else, she brought humor to her spirituality. In a June entry she wrote:

> Dearest M.M.2, Today I'm thinking of Robert Frost's lines: "Forgive, Oh Lord, my foolish pranks on Thee, and I will forgive Thy great big one on me."—I'm always thinking, at least, I won't live long enough to have diseases of old age like tiny bladder, no teeth, or osteoporosis—wouldn't it be a scream, though, Mary, if I did?!!

And in a July entry she wrote:

> I have decided how I'm going to die: of my heart bursting in its cavity with love, joy, gratitude, <u>and</u> clear vision—if we could see it clearly, I know we would think it was funny, Mary, so my heart will burst with laughter, too . . .

M.M.'s humor never kept her from facing the truth of her illness. Instead, it seemed to support her courage to be open to its path. In an August entry she explained:

> The reason I'm so tired is because I'm about to make a consciousness change. I must concentrate on what that change is, and let my higher Self take care of the form, for it is always the form that makes me afraid. The important thing is, that in dying there is no death. That will be my only reality.

As I read through to the end of M.M.'s book, her clear, direct words, so funny and so full of love for me, allowed me to open without fear to her suffering and to the reality of her impending death, and they offered me a new perspective on death. Even her drawings played that role. She would place a hilarious self-portrait on the page facing an entry that described her struggle with her declining body. When she wrote of a life-threatening hemorrhage she suffered that September, she placed an exquisitely detailed drawing of a flowering begonia on the facing page. Her little book was a hand held out to me, showing me how to live and how to dare to look at death—always in full relation to the humor, beauty, and joy that remain on the path.

M.M. lived for five months after she sent me her completed book. In her final entry she says:

> Dear Mary, I found the secret to life at last. "The only way you can ever bring about this change in thinking is by first changing your attitude towards all these things you now think are not what they ought to be . . . for who is the master, your body, your mind, or You, the I AM within?" (*The Impersonal Life*.) So Mare, I repaired to my bedroom to meditate and figured the most perfect vision I'd ever had of myself was teaching yoga to the entire Israeli army and teaching every single resident of that country to drop all they're doing at nine o'clock p.m. and chant *Shalom* for fifteen minutes, and the combined vibrations of all that brings Peace, needless to say, to the Middle East, and in turn, to the world. So that is Me, the *Real Me* . . . and I know the *Real You* . . . because that spark of divinity lights

you up so thoroughly that you cannot hide your love of light and peace and love . . .

. . . And here traileth off the tortured ramblings of me to you . . . with a wink and a smile. Love—M

P.S. "It is not necessary that anyone should remember that we have ever lived. All that means anything is that while we live we LIVE, and wherever we go from here, we shall keep on living." (Ernest Holmes)

Mary Margaret's mother understood how much we loved each other. She allowed me to speak to M.M. on the phone shortly before her quiet and peaceful death. In hushed whisperings, we touched each other's heart. Beneath the sadness, I knew she would not leave—that she would remain in my heart, and she did, preparing me for my own deep journey.

CHAPTER TWELVE

ANOTHER SEA CHANGE was happening within. It started in the months following Mary Margaret's death, while I was teaching a course on graphics in journalism at the School of Visual Arts. It began with discomfort in my left arm. At first the symptoms seemed related to a mild tendonitis in my elbow that I'd gotten from playing tennis. But after I stopped playing, the pain increased. It took over my entire arm and moved up through my shoulder. Soon I couldn't raise my hand above my neck. The doctor diagnosed it as a frozen shoulder. He couldn't relate it to the tendonitis, nor could he give me a cause. After several months of extremely uncomfortable physical therapy, I regained the normal range of movement. It took several more weeks for the pain to subside.

My knees had also been giving me trouble, especially the left knee, which swelled up intermittently and became quite painful. During the episode with my shoulder, I experienced a severe flare-up and went to a knee specialist who prescribed crutches. He explained I had inherited a congenital condition in both knees. He added, however, that from the X-rays he couldn't see any reason for the pain and swelling to be focused in the left knee. During those next months, I developed other medical problems that curiously expressed themselves on the left side of my body. I never told the doctors that my left side felt more vulnerable than my right; that when it wasn't hurting, it didn't feel sentient or fully awake. A weird sense of dis-ease accompanied this realization. Rather than analyzing it, I pushed it from my mind.

At about the same time, within the nest of my home within our home, bouts of fear began to disturb and threaten my sense of safety and my feelings of connection to Tom. One weekend when we were alone, a growing sense of dread blossomed into an acute feeling that I was dying. My heart began to race, accompanied by a terrifying feeling of impending separation, of leaving the earth in a vortex of fear. I called out to Tom. We thought of calling 911, but instead I lay down on the floor in the bedroom and waited until it passed.

How could this be happening to me? I had successfully completed the therapeutic work around Father's death. I was expressing my individuality and feeling competent both within the environment of my home life and in interactions with the outside world, yet I now felt totally at risk. Nothing made sense. The panic and my fear of dying finally drove me to seek an appointment with my new internist, Dr. Brentwood. I had yet to meet this doctor whom I had inherited after my old internist retired. Reaching his nurse by phone, I was informed that the first available appointment was in three weeks. I pleaded with her to let me see the doctor earlier, telling her I needed help. With irritation in her voice, she informed me she would have to call me back.

The nurse called later that week and said she would fit me in the next day. On the dot of my eleven o'clock appointment, I was ushered in to see Dr. Brentwood. I found myself facing a tall, blank-faced man with steely eyes and coarse gray hair. He briefly stood behind his desk to shake my hand and pointed to the empty chair that faced him. Feeling apprehensive, I sat down, watching while he pulled himself up to his desk. His hands were unusually pale and large, with black hairs growing around the knuckles of his long fingers. He seemed to stiffen as he straightened in his chair.

"You are a new patient," he began. "Just to make myself clear from the beginning, I don't appreciate you pulling rank with your family name in order to obtain privileged treatment. I treat all my patients the same."

There was silence while I stared at him in disbelief. "I don't understand," I finally replied. "I never said anything to the secretary; I didn't even know you knew my family name."

He looked at me with exasperation, didn't answer, got up, and motioned for me to follow him to an examining room. After the examination I went back into his office. He told me everything looked normal, especially on my left side, but he needed to wait for the results from the blood tests.

"By the way," he asked, "what would you describe as your main symptom, your main complaint?"

I hesitated. I heard my voice, as if from a distance, saying, "I think I am going to die."

Dr. Brentwood shook his head and laughed. "Really? That's unlikely—the best thing for you to do, Mrs. Morgan, is to see a psychiatrist and get out of the house. If you have any skills, you might think of getting a job."

"Screw you!" I muttered, slamming the door as I got into a cab. My eyes smarted with tears. Any fear died right then in the anger. No way would I go back to him. If there was nothing wrong with me physically, I'd tough it out.

"And screw you again," I thought. "I *have* a job."

CHAPTER THIRTEEN

<hr>

IT FEELS AMAZING to me that a relationship as life sustaining and nourishing as mine was with Tom could come to an end. Perhaps Tom and I were meant to come together with important gifts for each other and then to part.

This thought brings me back to an afternoon's conversation on a beach in Nassau in 1978. Tom and I were spending a long weekend there at a friend's house, trying to gain some perspective on the inevitability of our magazine's closing—to make a plan for that process and to discuss what to put in the last issue. It was a sad time for both of us. We held hands as we walked barefoot in the damp sand, the day fading before us into a gray sea. It felt like a whole chapter in our lives was ending. At the same time, I held a deep conviction that within its two-year life span we had accomplished a lot with *Politicks*.

Tom and I reminisced as we walked along the beach sharing stories about the wonderful group of writers and artists that had flourished at

Politicks and who would surely go on to promising careers. I told him I knew that it couldn't have happened without him as editor. We talked about the two prizes we had won and the gallery show of our graphics. I shared with him my pride in his contributions to social and political activism and my respect for his concern for the welfare of the staff by closing the magazine rather than failing to make payroll just so we could put out one last issue.

Despite this important conversation and other long talks, Tom took the full weight of responsibility for the termination of our magazine and felt he had let down our investors and our staff. I tried to engage his natural enthusiasm and optimistic spirit as we implemented the plan for the closing process, but it became increasingly clear that his spirit was damaged by our venture's impending end.

Although he didn't share this with me, I sensed he saw *Politicks'* demise as a professional and personal failure. I kept reminding myself that I could not know or fully understand his position; however, I could not suppress my pride and pleasure in what we had accomplished together. We both knew that few, if any, political magazines survive without large and continuous infusions of money—money that we didn't have. I took that to heart. I wanted us to move on together to something new. But after *Politicks* closed, our paths diverged. Tom left the world of editing and journalism and never returned. He began the long, solitary process of writing his second novel, a project he had deferred for years. A job I thought I had gotten at the *Daily News* fell through. I went on to teaching a course in graphics and journalism at the School of Visual Arts.

During our marriage, Tom had consistently acknowledged me as a person, not a Rockefeller; he had recognized and supported my competence, and helped me to grow. Now I wanted to fly on my own. I moved from thriving under a mentor-mentee relationship to craving more mutuality and independence. Sadly, it was not possible for us. Our intimacy and sharing slowly waned, replaced with a developing sense of distrust and conflict. Significant issues developed on both sides. We spent four years in couples' therapy trying to address them. The effort was unsuccessful.

Despite my newfound sense of independence and stubborn effort to repress my feelings, my fear of death and the numbness and pain in my left side remained, diminished but still lurking in the background. Tom and I both experienced major losses during this period—for me, the death of my father and of Mary Margaret. As we grew apart, these painful transitions were experienced and endured separately, exacerbated by different frames of reference. The beautiful intimacy we had shared slowly died. Our nest within our apartment began to feel like a prison. One morning I woke up knowing we could not mend the split. Tom felt the same. We mutually agreed to separate early in the winter of 1987, after fifteen years of marriage.

I can hear the scratching of Tom's old-fashioned pen as he signed our separation agreement. I had always loved this pen's distinctive sound and delighted in the fact that all his letters and notes to me were written with a pen using ink drawn from a glass bottle. Now that pen, as it scrolled his name, broke the contract of our fifteen-year life together. My signature ended it. The lawyer, Tom's cousin and our friend, gathered up the separation agreement papers. We left Tom's new apartment together—I filled with sadness, the feeling of failure, and the familiar sense of fearful isolation. Tom would not follow. He had already packed his things and moved forever from our home.

Although all were grown and two were living on their own, my children were deeply affected by the failure of our marriage. Sabrina had just finished a college sabbatical working in Nepal. She had arrived home bursting with enthusiasm and news. I had never seen her so joyous or with a clearer sense of purpose for her life. I dreaded telling her of our pending separation and will always remember with sadness her beautiful face when I imparted the news. Her expression went blank; then her face seemed to break like the spreading pattern of a car windshield when hit with a significant blow. There were no pieces to pick up. They had fallen inward.

I held to our decision to divorce with deep regret, for my children had come to trust in our marriage. They had made it part of their lives and had grown to love Tom as a second father. At the same time, it was clear to me that this decision provided the only way forward for my life.

CHAPTER FOURTEEN

THE NEXT YEAR, I bounced between energetic relief and aching lone-liness that haunted the early hours before I got going with my day. Interwoven with a childlike feeling of isolation and abandonment were a sequence of dreams I could not get my mind to remember. I scrambled to fill the untenable vacuum inside. It was as if this roiling void, which so loudly echoed the end of an intimate bond, could not stand its own emptiness and quickly spawned another union. This time, however, the relationship did not evolve into a marriage, but remained for its duration an all-consuming love affair.

I had known Jeremy for three years before breathlessly awakening to him in full-blown physical attraction. One day I noticed how he moved. When he got up or turned around or reached for something, all parts of his body flowed together in smooth simplicity. This interrelationship of parts seemed to go beyond his body as if it was attached to his mind and spirit; nothing stood in the way of the flow. He gave direct, accessible messages to the world around him. When he communicated with me, I knew where I stood. Words never came with a double agenda, and I sensed he had no interest in my status or family. We worked together in a simple, straightforward, and harmonious way. It soon became obvious that the electric attraction I experienced was mutual. We were not drawn to each other intellectually; we did not share the world of culture or ideas. Jeremy offered me an intensely masculine yet sweet desire that hinted at a deeper connection. Our attraction felt clear, pure, and uncomplicated.

As we became intimate, I embarked upon a glorious adventure. I felt I had known Jeremy before, for within the newness of our discovery, I experienced open excitement with no hesitation or shyness. Rather, an immediate sense of trust had created a jumping-off place for me from which I could journey and explore. New areas of delicious feeling announced themselves over the following weeks. I forgot the outside world.

Jeremy and I explored our love like two children on a treasure hunt of discovery. Outdoors, we found each other again and again: lying together in a hidden glen on a mossy floor, merging within the embrace of a pond's dark water, or just wandering through the woods, completed by the clasp of our hands. Indoors, after lovemaking, we would often curl up and take a nap. There, in Jeremy's arms, and just before sleep, I would have a strange yet exquisite experience. I experienced myself as a tiny being gently floating. Jeremy floated with me—two essences held within a vast, sweet, limitless completeness.

I did not share this waking dream, not even with my lover. I sensed that it came from a deeper and more private place than our bond, and might disappear if it were translated into words.

Our time together, filled with trust, excitement, and sharing, created a new kind of self-confidence that opened me to a wider experience of myself, especially in nature. Its beauty was deeply private. We did not share our outside lives; we explored the enclosed world of our own making, but it opened to a larger sense of connection that profoundly nourished me. Jeremy and I implicitly knew we would never marry. We came together from different backgrounds and our own separate worlds. We were powerfully drawn to share our love but not to build a sustaining relationship. We both knew we had unfinished lives to attend to: lives we could not ask each other to support. After two years, a moment came when we understood it was time to part. It was a mutually sad realization, but to me it also felt as if in a beautiful way, we had met each other's need to completion.

I wanted to mark the ending of our relationship, to honor the gift of Jeremy in my life. I suggested we spend a week in Rome, a city we had dreamed of visiting together. Jeremy had a break between jobs and agreed.

We arrived in Rome in the late spring. Scented blooms burst from city trees and filled the flower stalls, the air was clear and cool, and our hotel upgraded us to a spacious room with a view. Everything seemed perfect. However, soon after we arrived, the old anxiety and a free-floating sense of impending abandonment returned. It left me feeling helpless and with a sudden deep fear of our separation. Jeremy expressed whatever feelings he had about our imminent parting as stoic, determined energy for the daily plan. We visited the ancient Roman sites without excitement or enthusiasm; we had lost our mutual sense of discovery. Although Jeremy was affectionate, I sensed with dismay that he had already begun to rejoin his other life and had emotionally left "us" behind.

For a couple of hours each afternoon he made his business calls to the United States from the hotel. I found a little side-street café where I sat waiting for him, drinking cups of milky tea and holding on for dear life to myself by reading the little book Mary Margaret had made for me the year before she died. Her colorful drawings and wise, irreverent words allowed me to smile. I held on to her love and courage and pretended we were talking to each other.

On the last day of our trip it rained and we went to the movies. I cried through *Moonstruck*, barely making out the figure of my favorite star, Cher. Neither Jeremy nor I could face dinner at a restaurant when it was over. We went back to the hotel, where we packed and called for room service. The knowing, the joy, the sharing—the very fabric of our union—tore with each piece of clothing I put in my suitcase. Part of me collapsed in helpless resignation, yet another part stood firm, determined to hold on to our bond until we had to part. I prayed fervently for release from the dread of impending loss. My prayers were momentarily answered, for when we made love, I was fully present in our profound, simple connection one last time.

Our parting took place at the airport the next morning.

We had agreed to take separate planes back to the United States. Jeremy's flight left an hour before mine. I watched him turn and walk away from me through the gate. At that moment I knew I could not board my flight home. I could not cover up my anguish.

My closest friend from college lived in London with her husband. In desperation, I called her and asked if I could stay with her for a couple of days. I could hear the reluctance in her voice; it was obviously not a convenient time. But she heard the distress in mine and agreed to my visit. By the time I reached their home in Chelsea, eight hours later, the pain of separation was all-consuming. My dear friend was kind but clearly perplexed. Why was I so upset by an affair that my lover and I had both amicably agreed to end? I had no answer.

A warm bath in an old clawfoot tub held me most of the next day. I kept the spigots running to cover up my sobs. I held on to the side of the tub. My body wanted to sink, to fall apart in the water.

On the following evening, goaded by guilt and a remnant of social self-respect, I realized I would have to pull myself together to face my two friends and then return home. I made a plane reservation, and at four o'clock the next afternoon, I flew to New York.

———

AT HOME, I stamped on the grief, but it would not be totally suppressed. It awoke inside me in the early morning, before I could get my feelings under control. On the floor, I would stop my daily exercise routine and sit, rocking back and forth with pain. Often there were no tears, just a wrenching sense of loss and loneliness. Losing Jeremy felt less and less connected to these feelings. Bewildered, I realized I did not miss him, yet I could not identify my loss.

CHAPTER FIFTEEN

IN THE NEXT few weeks, shadowed dreams haunted restless nights, dreams that faded as I reached for them. During the day, I pushed away the recurring sense of loss; at the same time, my mind kept up a constant refrain: If it isn't Jeremy, what fuels my grief? One night lying in bed, alternating between reading and drifting toward sleep, my eyes closed. I could sense the floating . . . swaying . . . moving with a gentle sea—new, entwined beings as big as everything—existence complete in our arms . . .

I sat up with a shock. It is Michael I am floating with—not Jeremy. It is Michael I am connected to; Michael I have lost . . .

I flash to my little apartment, my hand moving unbidden over a blank sheet of paper: *"I am a twin."*

Part deeply relieved and part stunned at coming upon this unfinished reality repressed for so long, I now faced the same conflict I had experienced in Dr. Simmons's office twenty years before. I recalled his authoritative stance and the clear, hard look that he had given me as he directed me to move on—to live my life.

"You are only a fraternal twin, no closer to Michael than your other siblings are . . ."

My brothers and sister had long since accepted Mike's death and seemed to have moved beyond the pain of their loss. What about me? I *had* been living my life—but I had not been able to move on.

Between resentment at my shrink's iron-clad judgment—how could he pretend to know what it was like for me?—and the fear of what it would mean to face the broken bond with Michael, now that I had acknowledged my deep and continuing connection to him, my threatened mind navigated a middle path. I needed to find some outside explanation for my feelings, some way to put them in perspective. Maybe then they would go away. I realized I knew very little about other twins. During my childhood summers in Maine, I had played with twin girls but lost touch with them after we grew up. My relationship with these girls had been easy and comfortable, and I took their closeness to each other for granted. They were identical twins, but what about fraternals? I wanted to know more. For six months, I immersed myself in the twin research of the 1980s. After reading everything I could get my hands on, three findings stood out—almost shouting at me—from my exhaustive notes:

- The early nurturing environment for twins sets the tone, quality, and intensity of the twin bond beyond the issue of whether the twins are identical or fraternal.

- Male and female twins carry out their separate gender roles while at the same time maintaining a strong, underlying connection and deep loyalty to each other.

- It is not unusual for fraternals to have deeply bonded relationships.

These findings brought validation and flooding relief. One book, *The Psychology of Twinship* by Ricardo Ainslie, discussed the issue of twin identity—how the twinship itself presents twins with the difficult developmental challenge of acquiring a separate and cohesive sense of self, a challenge that is sometimes not met. I remembered the struggle I had had in finding myself in relationship to my family and to my father. Had developing an early sense of identity also been a problem for me because I was a twin? A distinct image of Michael and me as babies formed: two tiny "I's" curled up together in the frame of a "we." The image of our floating together followed, bringing up the fear and the shadow of pain.

For a couple of days I stopped reading. I tried to focus on my practical life. But I could no longer accept not knowing, not feeling, and being guided by others who had no personal experience from which to make a judgment. There was no protective fog. Some deep imperative had surfaced from within that now pushed me forward. I searched for anything written on the subject of grief and twinless twins. I found nothing.

Rod holding me, Mom holding Michael, Steven watching and Father taking family photo, Spring 1938

Me and Mike (right) in our outdoor nap crib, Pocantico, 1939

Mom with Michael and me (right), first portrait, 1939

Photo by Lena G. Towsley

Playing in the rock garden, Pocantico, 1940

Summer in Maine 1940

In our double carriage with Pat, Central Park, 1940

Summer in Maine, 1940

Photo by Lena G. Towsley

Mike tree-climbing, Pocantico, 1945

Me, painting, Pocantico, 1945

Photo by Ilse Bing

Ann's Wedding, Pocantico, 1955

Harvard Graduation, June 1960

Vassar graduation, June 1960
Photo by John Lane Studio

Mary and Michael—coverage of Father's Governorship, 1958
Photo by Barrett Gallagher–Barrett L. Gallagher photographs and film collection, #3956,
Division of Rare and Manuscript Collections, Cornell University Library.

Michael and me, summer on the coast of Maine, 1960

Michael taking his turn paddling in the Asmat, 1961
Photo by Samuel Putnam

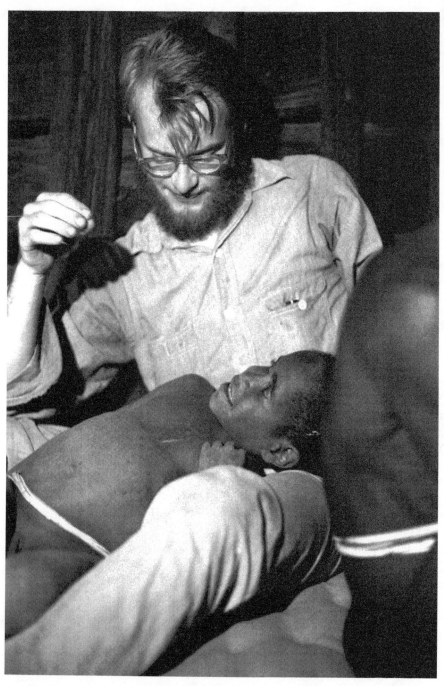

Mike playing with a little boy in his lap, Asmat, 1961

A plane searches swamps of New Guinea for Michael Rockefeller, 1961

Photo by Eliot Elislofon, Time Life Pictures/Getty Images

Press Conference, Merauke, 1961

AP/London

Mouth of Eilandan River, where Michael's boat capsized, Asmat, 1961
Photo by Eliot Elisofon, Time Life Pictures/Getty Images

CHAPTER SIXTEEN

—————————

SO WHAT ABOUT Michael and me—our beginnings as twins? Mother and my old nurse Pat knew more about our early lives than anyone else. Both readily agreed to be interviewed.

Mother's enthusiasm and open-hearted answers to my questions surprised and touched me. She could have easily closed the door to that part of her life rather than risk re-exposure to so much loss. Instead, her memories seemed to enable her to touch a treasured experience of early motherhood. I taped our conversation.

Mother began with, "You remember my story, Mary—neither I nor the doctor knew I was having twins. Well, I *certainly* had a very uncomfortable pregnancy. I had a lot of pressure and fainted *all* over New York City. Three weeks before I was due, the doctor felt one head low down in my pelvis and a heartbeat high up, too far from the head to make sense. He told me he wanted me to have an X-ray.

"After the procedure, the nurse ran in. Pointing at my stomach, she cried, 'Oh, Mrs. Rockefeller, you are a very lucky lady! There are two babies in there!'"

I caught the excitement of Mom's dramatic rendition and her perfect imitation of the nurse's Irish accent.

"Wow. What did you think?"

"I didn't know what to think. I didn't know what to say or what to believe. I asked to see the pictures and there you were, as clear as anything—both of you babies with your heads down, one low in the pelvis and one high up.

"The doctor saw that I was overwhelmed. He told me not to worry because you each weighed over five pounds and were healthy babies, carried almost to full term. That was a great comfort to me, Mary." She paused, remembering, and then said, "When I went into labor, Michael was born first."

"Were there any problems?"

"No. I had a healthy, normal labor, but I had no anesthesia because of the risk with bearing twins, and I was absolutely exhausted after Michael was born. I went into my second labor almost immediately with the worst pain. You didn't budge."

"I'm sorry, Mom. That must have been terrible . . . maybe I wanted to stay there," I added as an afterthought. "You know, I finally had enough room. I can see myself stretching out my arms and legs and then snuggling in." We both laughed.

Mom continued. "When I told the doctor I was exhausted, he put me out and they took you with forceps. When I came to, there you were— one boy and one girl. It was all totally overwhelming, Mary. I mean, it was about the most exciting thing that ever happened to Daddy and me. We were *utterly thrilled*."

Held in the awe of that moment, Mom and I fell silent.

She then went on to describe our being brought from the hospital to live at our country house in Pocantico Hills. It was the same trip she had taken with her three other newborns.

"You all were what Granny Clark called 'my spring lambs,' brought out to enjoy your first months on the green lawn in the warm sun with the birds singing amid the new leaves. And it was so lovely with you two little ones just down the hall." She smiled at the memory.

I asked Mother if we were close as babies.

"Oh, you were very close and very happy as long as you lay near each other. You spent a couple of hours outside each day in the kiddy coop—you remember, the white outside crib with the screened sides and top?

"Well, we copied the small Aldrich family crib for indoors, to make two of them, but you both cried when you were separated, so we had to find one big crib. You slept in it together until you were over two and Michael climbed out."

Mom stopped and thought a bit. "One of my fondest memories, Mary, was the first time you saw each other—now, I mean that you physically recognized each other. One day you were both lying on the big bed in my room, and one of you reached out to the other. Then it wasn't long before you started to smile at each other, and from then on it was totally fascinating to watch the two of you interact. You were always close together. It was really very cute and divine. You know, no ordinary baby sees another baby. They see a sibling come in or a friend when they are bigger, but when they are teensie they never see another teensie being like themselves, a tiny being who is always there and seems to teach them about themselves."

Mom's words touched a sweet, wordless place in me. They invited tears, which I quickly suppressed.

———

LIKE MY MOTHER, my old nurse Pat was in her early eighties at the time I interviewed her. When I tracked her down, she was living in a nursing home outside Burlington, Vermont; I had not seen her for over ten years. She was thrilled to meet with me, to catch up on my life, and to reminisce about Michael. Although frail in body, her mind had remained clear and her opinions as sharp-edged as they had been when I was a child.

Pat had entered our lives when we were nine months old, first taking care of Michael and me, and later minding my older siblings as well. She left to become my cousins' governess when Michael and I reached the age of ten.

The information Pat shared during our conversation corroborated much of what my mother had said: We were extremely close and well-adjusted babies, happy in nature except when we were separated. She told me Michael and I played side by side until Michael learned how to walk. He was eager to explore. Before tottering across the room, he would gather up our toys to take with him. I would screech in protest. Despite such disruption to our play, it took me several more months before I tried to walk.

"You were so frustrated when Michael took your toys," Pat remembered. "One time you actually bit his arm."

I asked her about our relationships with other children and our first experiences in school. She explained that our little world together seemed so complete that Mother did not make a special effort to bring other children over to play. After we moved to Washington, D.C., we went for a couple of hours each week to a small informal play group at the home of a friend. At four, we were sent to the Beauvoir Nursery School.

I shared a memory of finger-painting at nursery school with Pat. Like the other schoolchildren, Michael and I were each given separate paints and sheets of paper. I left mine and joined Mike, both of us on our knees, our fingers oozing in and out of each other's grasp as we slapped the paper and pushed the delicious colored liquid out over the white sheet. Soon, the teacher came over and made me leave Michael and go back to my place. I sat and stared at the paper and the paints. Alone, I had no sense of what to do or what to make.

"That *was* a problem," Pat said. "We often had difficulty getting you to engage in any endeavor without your brother."

Pat's stories opened up a raft of fleeting memories. That night I had trouble sleeping. When I got home, memories of Michael and our life together pervaded the day. Each memory came with ominous longing and the threat of uncontrollable grief. The sense of danger closed off these thoughts and the possibility of any more, but at the same time, it felt safe to think about Mike's close friends—Sam, Wat, John, and Saky. They had become my friends as well, and I had dated two of them in high school and college. We had spent weekends and summer visits together. Now they were married, had families of their own, and lived in different cities. Although I did not see them often, we had kept in touch since Michael's disappearance. Suddenly, I longed to recreate the special bond we had once shared. On the spur of the moment, I called and invited them for a weekend reunion at my home in the country. They all seemed delighted with the idea, but with family and business responsibilities, only Sam and John were able to come.

We gathered on a Friday night, falling into easy, affectionate cama- raderie—laughing and sharing stories about our times together with Michael. Saturday morning we rose at sunrise, put my canoe on top of John's car, and drove to a nearby lake. Because it was a state reservoir, no canoeing was allowed. Flat-bottomed boats were OK because they would not easily tip over. We decided we were all good paddlers; tipping over was not our problem. Laughing and whispering, we furtively slid the canoe into the water, paddling in stealthy silence in and out of the mist that surrounded the small protective islands in the middle of the lake. We kept an eye out for the Water Patrol boat and listened for the sound of its reprimanding megaphone. It never appeared. Our delight was infectious—it was as if we had reentered our teenage years.

We were not drawn to share our present lives. For the entire weekend, we continued to recreate the environment that had held us together with Michael. My twinship felt acknowledged and embraced.

———

"Listen, Geedie," Michael says, leaning toward me over the heavy high-backed wooden benches that line the walls of the Back Bay railroad station in Boston. "We have a bit of a change in our plans—it won't be a problem, though."

I can tell by the twitch on the right side of his mouth that it might very well be a problem and if so, it will be more mine than his, for he's already finding the situation funny. I look at my watch. It's 9 pm on Saturday, the last night before the end of Christmas vacation. I'm hungry and tired. I've spent the past few minutes thinking of how I'm going to get the homework done that I didn't do over the holidays. The eight-hour trip from Vermont's Mad River ski area on a train without a dining car has tried all our patience—that is, all except Mike's, who as usual seems disconnected from the annoyance of everyday inconveniences. Meme, my college roommate, and I are both looking forward to a hot bath and a good night's sleep in our room at the Hotel Charles in Cambridge. We will take another train in the morning to New York City, then on to Vassar College in Poughkeepsie. Mike and his roommates, Wat, Sam, and Saky, are going straight to their dorm at Harvard.

"What kind of a change in plans?" I ask Michael warily, watching the upward tilt at the corner of his mouth.

"Well, Sam just phoned the dorm to find out if it's open, and if not, where Mr. Stevens would leave us the key. But Mr. Stevens told him the freshman dorm would not be open until tomorrow morning. No one is allowed to stay there tonight."

Looking delighted and sheepish all at once, Michael continues, "We all thought you and Meme would help us out and let us stay with you in your room tonight."

I look over at Meme and then back at Mike. "You're kidding!"

The rise in my voice jolts Meme out of her book. She jumps in: "Stay

WHEN GRIEF CALLS FORTH THE HEALING

in our room? You guys are nuts. The hotel won't allow single men in women's rooms—if we bring you up there, we'll all get kicked out."

"No way, Geedie," I add. "Just forget the whole idea. You have to figure something else out. We had to leave our parents' phone numbers when we reserved the room. If there's a problem, they'll call home—can you imagine Mom if she found out?"

"You don't know my mother," Meme echoes.

Sam, Wat, and Saky appear around Mike. It is clear from their eager looks they have decided that our room is the solution.

"Let's just check it out," Saky says with his most charming smile. "Mike could help Mary with the bags. If the coast is clear, he'll hide in the bathroom in your room and then Sam can make the next trip with the rest of the bags while Wat distracts the porter with your skis, which have to go in the baggage room. In the meantime, Sam joins Mike in the bathroom and Meme's at the desk checking in and distracting the desk clerk. When Wat's finished, he will sneak up the back stairs. I'll go get the pizza and be the deliveryman."

We argue back and forth, Meme and I protesting until we are worn down. Meme gives in first; I can tell she's interested in Sam. We agree to Saky's plan. But first, I'll go ahead and check out the lobby.

"One final thing," I say, looking at Mike. "Meme and I get the beds and you guys get the floor or the chairs and the sofa if there is one."

Grumbles and laughs and "Oh, okay, if that's the way you feel" follow as we pick up our bags, check the boys' skis at the railway station's storage room, and head out for the short taxi ride to Cambridge.

I suppose we are in luck. The Charles, a rather rundown place, but the only real hotel in town, is having some sort of mini convention. The small staff looks overworked and preoccupied. Saky's plan is perfect and we carry it through without a hitch. He even borrows the pizza parlor's delivery hat and sails up the elevator with our dinner.

In a million years, I'd never think of sleeping with a bunch of boys in a hotel room. Yet, Mike's kind of right, it is really fun sneaking them all upstairs and having a pizza picnic on the floor. We find two extra pillows in the closet, and Mike and Sam say they'll use their duffel bags to put under their heads. We talk and laugh until after midnight. Meme and I share the bathroom first, then it's the boys' turn—no hot baths for anyone or getting undressed.

I'm just drifting off to sleep when I hear Mike's whisper at the side of my bed, "Move over, Geedie." I inch over to the edge of the single bed and let him in beside me. He's rolled up a towel for his head.

"You're crazy, Geedie," I whisper.

Happy in some instinctive way, we shove each other a bit until we feel comfortable.

"What about tomorrow morning?" I whisper again. "I'm going to look like hell."

"Pretend it's like camping," Michael yawns. "No one cares."

"I suppose you're right . . . We had fun, didn't we, Mike?" He doesn't react. I can tell from his breathing, he doesn't hear me—he's already asleep.

Bathed in leaf-filtered light and in the fullness and warmth of the late spring day, I waved goodbye to John and Sam and watched their two cars move around the circle of the driveway. With a final crunching sound of gravel, they entered the hedgerow of trees and disappeared.

The open, sensate beauty of the moment suddenly dissolved. My balance faltered and failed. Grabbing for the handle on the door of the garden wall, I stared through the wall opening trying to shake the dizziness. Minutes before, the encircling flowers had greeted me with glowing hues and mingling scents. Now they appeared pale and flat, as if caught in an overexposed photograph.

Trying to orient myself, my thoughts scrambled to the present. Then it hit me—for the first time in my life, I was truly alone—no husband, no lover, no job, and my children were grown. My life spread before me—a great blank.

Oliver, my yellow Lab, perfectly grounded in the beautiful day, walked happily beside me while I stumbled back into the house. At the kitchen table, my hands propped up my head. The dizziness slowly cleared. I ached with loss. My chest hurt. A fearful place swelled within— too late to turn away. I knew it was Michael—I had to let him go from my life! I didn't even know what that meant, but the fearful declaration pressed to be heard. There wasn't time! Somewhere there had to be a safe place where I could listen.

Oliver padded over to his bowl, lay down and looked up at me, asking to be fed. His sweet request lifted me from the dire inner warning.

As I fixed his food, I had an idea.

Two years earlier, my sister Ann had described an annual two-week transformational experience that takes place in wilderness areas of the Rocky Mountains. She was in training to become one of their guides. "Returning to Earth" encompasses seven days of preparatory group work at a rural retreat center, followed by seven days of wilderness living, including four days of fasting in solitude. The program is modeled on the traditional Native American "vision quest," in which a brave or chief would leave his tribe and go into the wilderness to seek a vision that would reveal a path for personal transformation during a period of uncertainty or transition. Behind the "Returning to Earth" vision quest lies the idea that by spending time alone relating to nature, a person could open a connection to his or her true essence and inner wisdom, a connection often obscured by daily responsibilities to family, tribe, or group.

The "Returning to Earth" experience had been adapted to modern Western life and was now led by three psychologists. After careful psychological and physical preparation and attention to forming a supportive participant group, the questers embark on a four-day wilderness solo.

Quite by accident, the brochure had surfaced in the bottom drawer of my desk. When my sister had given it to me, it seemed like a wonderful experience—for someone else. I had never carried a thirty-five-pound pack or attempted to camp on my own. My camping experience consisted of riding on horseback as a child with my family up into the Teton Mountains of Wyoming, accompanied by a cook, pack horses carrying supplies, and cowboys who acted as guides and tent builders. I had never even built my own campfire—just sat around one at dusk, singing western songs and toasting marshmallows.

While I was rereading the brochure that night at the kitchen table, my reaction was quite different. Over the years I had increasingly experienced the beauty of the natural environment and had delved into its compelling mystery with Jeremy. "Returning to Earth," within the context of a professionally guided group, seemed perfectly suited to my need for solitude and support, while I opened to and allowed my feelings. Still, surviving alone for four days in the wilderness felt like a huge challenge.

Oliver looked up at me, his tail gently thumping the floor. It was as if he understood what I'd been thinking. His clear, brown eyes seemed to be saying, "It's safe; you'll see." I slid down from my chair onto the floor next to him, taking his head in my lap. *I am not alone*, I thought.

CHAPTER SEVENTEEN

MAY SLIPPED INTO June. With a rapidly beating heart, I called Ann to find out if there was any room on the July "Returning to Earth" vision quest. Someone had just dropped out. I filled out the long application and sent it in. Part of me hoped I would not be accepted. The bigger part knew my joining the group was a foregone conclusion.

The acceptance letter came two weeks later. It outlined our schedule, listed what we would need for the quest, and described our base—a small, rustic meditation center in the foothills of the San Juan Mountains, a couple of hours from Telluride, Colorado. We would spend the first week there before going up into the mountains for the wilderness experience. I moved about in a motivated daze, buying and assembling the required gear on the equipment list. Pleasure, even a kind of giddy excitement, accompanied my efforts, the feelings a child might have in assembling things she would need for a night in a tree house or for a camping adventure in the backyard with her pals. I packed and repacked my huge blue backpack. It was still two weeks before I would leave.

About a week before the trip I awoke in a full-blown panic. By midday I called Ann and told her I had decided not to go. Previously I had shared with her that the reason for wanting to make this quest centered around my not having gotten over the death of Michael. Now I explained to her in a thinly controlled voice, that in the last month I had felt much better about Michael's death and really didn't think the experience fit any longer. Ann did not relate directly to my defensive excuse. Instead, she wisely suggested that I speak directly to Sam Jenkin, one of the quest's leaders. She would give him my number and ask him to call.

The tone of Sam's voice on the phone was friendly and direct. I skipped the reasons I had given Ann and simply told him the truth that I did not think I could handle the solo. I failed to mention that I did not feel up to taking the trip.

"It is about making my camp so far away from the others. Being alone and without food in the wild for four days—I've never done it before."

"The leaders will remain at our base camp throughout the solo period," Sam replied. "And we will have two days to help you prepare before you go out. I suggest you take it one step at a time, Mary. If you still feel the same way when it is time to leave for your solo, you can spend the nights with us at base camp and go for one-day solos or spend as much time alone as you can tolerate. I don't think anyone will have a problem with that."

The strong thrust of my negative reasoning began to weaken. My resolve then collapsed like a pair of windless boat sails. In that moment, I felt so tired it was impossible to muster up another excuse. Sam asked if he had addressed all of my concerns. "I think so," I said.

"Will you come?" His tone was open and reassuring.

"Yes."

CHAPTER EIGHTEEN

MEREDITH LITTLE AND Steven Foster's guidebook *The Sacred Mountain: A Vision Quest Handbook for Adults* describes a preparatory ceremony for all participants to complete before leaving on their journey. The Medicine Walk entails a six-hour solitary meandering walk in a natural, unoccupied setting. One is asked to enter this place on foot before sunrise and to wander at the will of one's intuition. "Be aware if you are feeling drawn to anything or in any particular direction. Listen and sense the consciousness of all that is around you. The Medicine Walk maintains connection with the beauty of life and the reality of death as both are reflected by the world of nature. At a certain point you will find one thing—a symbol of meaning and importance to you. This one thing must return with you and become the symbol of your vision quest."

The guidebook goes on to suggest that the walker perform a simple ceremony of gratitude to nature and to the earth, both at the beginning and at the end of the day's journey. Finally, it asks that one bring along a journal to record experiences and impressions, and to bring along plenty of water but to forego food.

I chose the Ward Pound Ridge Reservation, a preserve of three thousand acres of woodland trails and meadows. It was not far from where I lived in Westchester County, New York. Interpreting the guidebook's use of the term solitary to mean not going with another human being, I took Oliver along for support.

At 4:30 a.m. we set forth. The headlights of my car illuminated the empty toll booth at the entrance to the reservation. Uncertain about entering the park before it officially opened at eight, I remembered I had noticed some rudimentary stone cabins at the edge of some of the trails on previous hikes. If camping is allowed, I rationalized, then campers must have permission to go in and out at any hour. Driving through the entrance, I followed the only macadam road, which bisected the reservation and ended in just over a mile at a parking area near a stream, picnic spot, and several trailheads.

Pulling into the parking lot, I turned off the engine and sat. Oliver's panting was the only sound to break the predawn stillness. The Medicine Walk fell outside the bounds of any previous experience, yet it fascinated me. I remembered the tiny lizard on the corrugated tin wall of the Quonset hut in Subic Bay. There, one of nature's small beings had reached out to me and had become my sustaining friend. At the same time, the reasoning world had dismissed my inner life—disallowing the strange and powerful tie I felt to my twin and the protracted pain of my loss that lay at the foundation of my being. Maybe these fields and rocks and trees beyond the car—if they were indeed conscious, as some physicists said—maybe they would know me. Maybe nature would guide and help me to heal.

I slid off the front seat and stood in the dark. My hand felt for and turned the back door handle to let Oliver out.

MEDICINE WALK JOURNAL JULY 1988

4:50 a.m. Oliver stays next to me; he seems to sense my uneasiness. Dripping trees surround us. One star in the sky, ground fog, and the beginning of faint glowing light. There are no lights from other cars—the reservation seems deserted.

5:15 a.m. Light begins to rise through fog. A bird sings, then a whole chorus. We walk back along the road to opening fields. Misty light throws the trees into silhouette; the hills beyond are overlapping one another, receding downward.

We've entered the woods—I wander along a stream. The water surface dances with bugs as if it's raining, but the sounds come from dripping trees which emerge now, one by one with the rising light. Birdsong is gentle.

I'm confused about the Medicine Walk. My guidebook is back in the car. What did it say about death . . . ? I know I am to follow where I'm drawn to go and to try to let go of the outside world. In my mind I keep hearing the refrain, "You must let Michael go."

We walk away from the stream back along the road. I stop. An orange snail is crossing. A deer steps from the woods—Oliver barks, ready for the chase. The deer vanishes into the trees. We are both drawn after it, climbing a hill. Trees drip and crackle.

6:45 a.m. Damp, pungent smells come from the ground. I like the earth's breath.

Morning sun rises over a mowed and undulating field. An enormous oak stands alone in the middle. I approach it. I am alone on this reservation. Have I trespassed? Now that it's light, maybe I'll be caught. I take refuge under the huge oak. Its ancient trunk and body stand outside of time. On one side of the tree a turned and rounded hole indicates an old wound. A daddy longlegs rests on the lichened trunk.

An ant emerges from the hole on a mission. In the sunny field grass, spider webs spread out in squares—small, white napkins twinkling with dew. Fog hugs the surrounding hollows.

Hidden among the leaves at the base of the oak tree is an acorn, its smooth surface worn and pitted. I push the nut with my thumb; it holds firm in its case. Placing it in my pocket, I wonder if it's meant to be my symbol.

A little bee fly visits the tree. Swallows swoop over the field. Following their flight, my sight is jarred by a car. A plane flies high overhead. I look for a hiding place. Another car passes on the macadam road—the driver sees me.

I hurry to find a trail and then leave it to sit on some rock shelves, stained dark as the wet trees. An ancient earthquake must have heaved them up. Endless time.

My foot slips off the edge of a mossy rock as I climb, throwing me to my hands and knees. I look at my stinging, muddy palms. I'm so vulnerable. What if I had fallen and broken my ankle? The surrounding, tangled woods feel frightening, yet they are beautiful! Oliver looks up at me.

He won't be on my quest!

Don't go there. Look. Listen. Here, now in this moment.

Ferns touch my feet. A few fronds bounce intermittently up and down, hit by the drops of leftover rain.

I wander into high, soaking grass, lifting my face to the momentary warmth of the sun. Deer flies buzz my head. It's time for my hat. The sun appears, then fades, then comes again—spots glowing on trunks, leaves fading to gray.

Back on the earth trail I sit to retie my wet boots, hoping not to get a blister. It's only two days before I leave. How will they dry?

A bee fly lands on the end of my pencil. It feels peaceful here on my little earth-and-pebble patch. I think I will like the day part of my solo.

I need to pee. There is no one on the trail. I get up, walk a few feet, pull down my pants, and squat. The wind shakes water from the trees onto my bare back and butt. Out in the open, not even behind a bush—I am free!

Walking again—I find a few interesting stones.

Before me a leaf flutters and spirals to the ground—an oval and finely corrugated beech tree leaf. Brilliant fall yellow colors one side and brown the other, its dying half shrivels like a folded accordion. The brown has begun to seep into the golden half. Is this leaf Michael and me, or just me—one side shriveled and dying, the other trying desperately to stay alive and sun-filled? I hear a woodpecker's hollow sound. I'm certain—this leaf is the symbol of my quest. It will come with me on my solo.

10:05 a.m. Oliver and I make our way back to the brook where I started. I'm drawn upstream this time, moving along the bank until we come upon a large pool set between two groups of rocks. The low water makes only a gentle trickling sound as it moves over the stones and into the tiny pond. In its deeper setting, the stream quiets and stills. A jutting rock calls me to sit on its flat surface. In my hand now are three leaves— one red, one yellow, one green. Two leaves have turned early and left their trees. Life colored these leaves, not death. The green leaf is the part of Michael that didn't get to live.

Across the pool, near the bank, two identical rectangular rocks rise from the water, large flat-topped forms a foot apart and parallel to each other. Ancient stone coffins—enduring twin shapes.

Standing, I turn toward the two massive stones for my ceremony. Prayers of gratitude follow each leaf as they float to the water. Nature feels an awesome friend.

I turn to leave. A flash of soft color claims my attention. Two small pink single-petal roses hang low, suspended over the water. Their color glows against a backdrop of reflected light, shade, and moving green. I look around; there are no other flowers along the bank, but as my eyes travel to make out the extent of the wild rose bush, I see a third rose by itself, its pink blossom turned away. I search for its twin, and find it nestled deep within the delicate thorny branches. Each rose is pure in color, pure in shape—two roses are together; two apart.

PART THREE

The Healing

CHAPTER NINETEEN

A DREAM WOKE me on the morning of my trip to Colorado:

> *I'm trying to keep some animals from getting into the house—not sure what kind they are. I follow them as they disappear over the roof. Somehow I know if I stop them from going in one way, they will get in another. Now I find a bunch at the front door. I can't get my hands on them.*

Somehow my heavy pack and I made it onto the flight leaving from Denver for Montrose, Colorado. After settling into my seat, I looked up and down the aisle, trying to figure out if anyone else on the small plane could be part of the vision quest group.

They are probably all jocks, I mused, dejected and peeved at the thought—*all used to hiking and climbing and spending days at a time out of doors.* Skipping over any middle-aged people who looked anything like me, I scrutinized the younger passengers. An all-too-familiar fear and panic began to rise from my chest to my throat, and I abruptly stopped the search. The narrow, cramped plane bumped and dipped through the clouds above the mountain peaks, finally landing on a thin airstrip that ended on the tarmac outside the Montrose terminal.

I was greeted at the baggage area by a young man who introduced me to our group, which had slowly started to gather. I noticed that several questers seemed to be my age, and two looked even older. One lady dragged her large pack over the floor from the baggage claim to where we were standing, as if she had never even tried to lift it. I felt profoundly relieved by her actions. If she dared to become a quester, I thought, so could I.

The van ride took two hours. The meditation lodge, our home for the next seven days, stood on a flat plain surrounded by groups of cottonwood and aspen trees. Sage brush and larger bushes dotted the dry, grassy ground. In the distance rose the hills and peaks of the San Juan Mountains, the site of our wilderness quest.

A rambling wooden structure formed the lodge. Standing ready to greet us at the front door were Steve Gallegos, Sam Jenkin, and Mel Bucholtz, the three psychologists and group leaders, joined by my sister Ann. Ann was there to support the leaders in their work and to guide the outdoor ceremonies. Her reassuring presence, as we piled out of the three vehicles, helped me quickly warm to the enthusiastic smiles of the leaders and the more tentative and shy smiles of the other questers I hadn't yet met.

Ann led us into the lodge and through the meeting hall, a large, rectangular space with mats and pillows grouped along its wooden floor. The hall opened to a row of small rooms where we would be sleeping. Each room contained two beds and two bureaus. My assigned roommate, Alice, a heavy-set, closed-faced woman in her mid-forties, entered our room ahead of me. She immediately put her things down on the left-side bed. She turned and drew an imaginary line down the center of the room with her finger.

"Everything to the left of this line is my side," she announced in a preemptive tone. "Keep your things on your side, and we won't have any problem being roommates."

During the time spent in that little room I kept to my side and to myself. My roommate's rigid boundaries reinforced my sense of isolation. Her cold, aggressive statement brought tears to my eyes. I felt at risk. The terror-filled place within had stirred awake and was starting to push against the walls constructed around it.

Our evening meal was simple and tasted fresh and good. We sat at wood tables, each seating six. There were fourteen questers besides me, twenty-two of us altogether, counting our leaders, a resident couple, and a woman who came in daily to help run the lodge.

Steve Gallegos, a short, stocky man with a neatly trimmed white beard, rose during the meal to welcome us. After warmhearted remarks, he let us know we would be gathering as a group in the meeting hall when the meal ended. Despite the friendly conversation and camaraderie at my table, his invitation stirred up my sense of growing risk. At the end of the meal, we washed our dishes in an assembly line, moving from three huge sinks of hot soapy water to pans of clear rinse water, to long drying racks into which we placed the clean dishes, glasses, and flatware. The warm water, the washing and rinsing, and the familiar clink and clatter of glasses and dishes momentarily calmed my fast-beating heart.

In the meeting hall, we gathered in a circle seated on the floor on the mats and pillows. Steve took the lead, asking each of us in turn to say our name and why we had decided to come on the vision quest. One after another, people began to share. My mind went blank:

I hear no names, no stories. It is my turn to speak. No words come. A dark roar gathers in my chest—sounds in my head. Huge water coming—forcing upward from the sea.

Ann's touch. Ann's presence. Her voice, finding me through the dark, through the roar.

There is a mat. She helps me down. Hands—so many hands, touching, holding me. Can't stop the water—rushing, rising in my throat, in my head.

"I am going to drown."

"No," came Steve's deep voice. "You will not drown, Mary. We are going to hold you. You can let go now. Let all the tears come out."

I knew who I wept for then—what the tears meant—no more searching, no more hoping. Michael was dead.

The group held me within their circle while I wept—so many, many tears for Michael held back for so long. The group held me until there were no tears left.

CHAPTER TWENTY

IN THEIR INTRODUCTION to *The Sacred Mountain: A Vision Quest Handbook for Adults*, Meredith Little and Steven Foster write of the traumatic transitions of modern life we are asked to face, survive, and grow from. They ask, "How many times in our span of years are we called upon to uproot and transplant, to let go of the old and embrace the new, to end it and go on, to plow under and plant the seed, to cease being ignorant and find out, to die and be reborn?" They describe the vision quest as an "experience of symbolically passing from one life stage to the next. The vision quester moves from the state of 'letting-go' to the state of 'new beginning.'"

Each of the seven days at the lodge involved preparation for the death of the former part of my life that no longer served, that place in me that I needed to be willing to let go before I could integrate my twin loss—before I could be reborn. Indoors and out, our group received teachings and took part in exercises and ceremonies. We shared and bore witness to each other's experiences. In our time together, we learned to listen to our inner voices, as reflected in the natural world around us and coming from deep spontaneous imagination. Through a series of guided imagery exercises, Steve Gallegos led us to places of inner wisdom. One morning, he asked us to find comfortable places on the mats in the meeting hall.

His deep, calming voice invites us to close our eyes. He guides us to feel connected with the earth below and the sky above. We are asked to receive their nourishment and support through our breath—breathing in nourishment as we inhale, and releasing what we no longer need with each exhalation. Feeling the support of the earth, we are asked to imagine roots growing from our body securing us in deep, rich soil.

Steve's voice helps me to spontaneously envision my roots, which grow down into the earth of my imagination, grounding me as if I were a tree. I gradually let go of my anxiety and begin to relax. I feel nourished and held by the earth and sky. I experience myself as the link between the two, as if I am the horizon. Now he asks us to imagine ourselves as a seed. I see myself as a tiny seed in the ground, a seed just beginning to split open, softened by spring rains and the warm soil. I observe myself as I begin to grow.

"What kind of plant are you becoming? Ask this plant if it has anything to show you or if it needs anything from you."

I hear no reply from the seedling, but somehow I understand it and what it wants. My plant is going to become a tree. I respond to its needs as it grows. It wants its branches untangled; it wants me to clear the ground around it so it has enough space in which to stretch its branches. As it moves and reaches upward, the little tree holds me; my arms embrace it, too. My tears become the gentle, warm rain that will help the tree mature.

Without words, the tree tells me that I must let Michael go from me now, from wanting him the way he was. I must do this for him as well as for me.

After some time, I opened my eyes. I was surprised to find myself surrounded by the quiet, reclining figures of the other questers. It was as if I'd been in another reality, and with the flick of a finger, had reentered the familiar one.

———

IN THE DAYS that followed, Steve helped me to further access and dialogue with deeper parts of myself through imagery exercises. Each time, his resonating voice led me out of the place of thinking into a state of deep relaxation, where I felt safely held and connected to the earth and sky and could call forth the voices of my inner knowing. Once he asked, "Do you love yourself enough to listen with the ears of your heart to the many voices of yourself speaking?"

In the second imagery journey, Steve called on us to focus our attention sequentially on seven different parts of our body, each representing a center within the body's energy system, also referred to as chakras. Each time we focused on a particular energy center, we were asked to invite an animal or guide to come forth. As it made itself known in our imagination, Steve would invite us to greet it and to make a relationship with it by listening to its needs and what it had to show us.

As I lay down, my mind filled with doubts and questions. *What if this is just some bizarre New Age nonsense? What if nothing happens, if no animals appear?* I knew I was jumping into a vast unknown space and I felt propelled to get up, to leave. But Steve's voice had begun the relaxation. Like a low, sonorous bell, it rang in the memory of the seed, the growing tree, and the feeling of its arms holding me as we were both nourished and anchored in the earth. I let go of the doubt and fear as I exhaled. I breathed in the sky's openness.

Steve moves my attention to the base of my spine. I become aware of the feelings and sensations of this area of my body. I'm more and more comfortable, resting my attention there. I call within this space for an animal guide and a large, coiled snake immediately appears as an image. I like snakes. She shows me her nest. She asks me to help her care for her eggs. Among the leaves of the snake's nest I find eggs that appear transparent. In one of them is a tiny version of myself. Together, the snake and I curl around her eggs to warm and hatch them.

Bringing my attention to the energy center in my stomach, I invite a guide and a brown rabbit appears, hopping around in the moonlight. It moves in and out of the sagebrush.

Its little body seems to say, "Have fun; be free."

"Aren't you scared?" I ask the rabbit. "You could be eaten by an owl if you dance under the moon like this."

"No," the rabbit replies. "I have no fear; I am friends with the Dove of Peace."

The rabbit asks me to wash its feet and scratch its soft belly, which I do.

When I invite an animal from my solar plexus, nothing happens. I wait and wait. In the background, my thinking whispers, Just make up an animal . . . maybe a bear! To my dismay, a large bat pops into my imagination. It flies in the dark to a pine branch above my head. I see its claws; light comes through the thin, ugly parchment of its wings. When I reluctantly greet it, it tells me it is my protector and will keep the nights free from negative energy on my vision quest solo. It stretches its wings and yawns, showing me its teeth. I know it wants a mouse to eat. I tell it I don't like the idea of killing anything. The bat looks nonchalant and seems bored with me, as if to say, "Get used to it, lady, that's what I do." Before I can react, it flies away.

Steve's voice draws my focus easily to my heart center. My heart swells and parts as if it were a curtain. Out of a deep, red glow comes a huge female elephant. She limps slightly. She asks if I will remove the stone that is embedded in her foot. I pry it out with a stick. She then curls her trunk around me and lifts me up, gently cradling and rocking me.

"I will be your friend and comfort you when you need me on your solo."

Her huge body and trunk encircle me with warmth and safety. She is my perfect mother. I don't want to leave her, and have a hard time following Steve's voice, which guides me to focus within my throat.

Out of my throat flies a tiny, iridescent white-and-blue-spotted butterfly. It asks for a drink. I offer it a flower filled with dew. It is exquisitely beautiful; I tell it so. Knowing it won't live long, I am sad. It shows me beauty is ephemeral.

When Steve's voice leads me to my head, all I see is fog. Finally, a coyote appears at one side by my ear. He trots around me, stops, cocks his head, and smiles. I don't trust him. Will this animal like me or bite me?

Coyote doesn't communicate or show me anything—just keeps watching me while its lips curl in a smile.

Finally, Steve guides us to the seventh chakra, to the space just above the crown of my head. An enormous black crow appears in the air above me and settles on a nearby tree stump. It comes to let me know that it will lift Michael's spirit up to the heavens when I am ready to let it go. The crow tells me that first, however, I must walk out with Michael through the "valley of death." When I ask the crow to explain this, I hear no reply. Fearful, I look for something reassuring in its gesture or in its face, but receive only the blank blackness within the outline of its shape. I look up toward the heavens. Far above, I think I see a dove.

This journey left me tired, vulnerable, and at the same time awed by the spontaneous magic that lay within me. With some apprehension, I wondered what it all meant and where the imagery journeys would take me.

Steve joined the table where I sat for lunch. Everyone wanted to talk about their animal guides and about their meaning and turned their chairs toward him to listen and join in.

"The animals are a way of accessing the deepest part of ourselves," he explained. "Don't analyze them with your thinking mind; instead, develop a relationship with them. Ask them questions; share your feelings. They will help you through the transformation that you've come here to make."

"What should we do," I asked, "if nothing happens when you guide us, if no images or animals come?"

A jolly look spread across Steve's bearded face. He seemed tickled by my question.

"*Nothing* is just an absence of *something*. You can be with that sense of nothingness and learn from it. You can ask it what it has come to show or tell you. Also, it might just need something from you." Steve laughed, and in our confusion and amazement, we caught his delight and joined in.

As I left the dining hall and set out on my afternoon walk, I mused over Steve's challenge to engage with the "nothing" place, to talk to it. When I dropped my initial skepticism, I found that this exercise actually made sense. Steve had such respect for the imagery process, a trusting acceptance of our journeys—an open curiosity. Maybe I could join that, just accept myself in all of the mysterious ways I was unfolding.

Wanting this feeling of openness and acceptance to include my relationships with the other questers, I tried to think of them all inclusively, leaving behind my critical inner voice. I tried to stop analyzing my behavior and the behavior of others and relaxed my sensitivity to whether the others liked me or not. Maybe they were all there to teach me about myself—like the animal guides, or like the yellow beech leaf with one half shriveled and dying. Maybe everyone and everything had a role to play in helping me to grow—if I could just open myself enough and trust.

With these thoughts, the image of Jim Baxter, another quester, came to mind, and with it, a warm and happy glow. I had liked Jim from the moment I met him. He stood about five foot ten with a slight, compact build, sandy brown hair, and a sensitive, open face. In his late twenties or early thirties, he was close to twenty years younger than me. We had begun talking in the van on the drive to the lodge. As we continued to meet and interact, we easily shared our stories and found we held the same desire to explore the meaning in our lives and to learn how we fit into the larger scheme of life. We sat next to each other in the circle of our gatherings, and had taken several walks together in our free time after lunch.

What is happening here, I thought. We have such a natural intimacy; we so easily understand and accept each other's feelings.

Abruptly, I saw Michael's face. I stopped my walk and sat down next to the path.

It was obvious. Why hadn't I seen it before? I had found Michael in Jim! He had the same build and height. His was a youthful, intelligent face like Mike's, expressing the same inquisitive and intense searching and sensitivity—he even seemed to have the same interest in sharing himself with me. And he wore glasses! Good God! I had opened myself to the grief and the finality of Michael's death, yet there I was, still looking for him and finding him in other people.

Uncovering these unconscious feelings and actions shook the confidence I had gained. I felt a huge distance between what seemed a never-ending need and my goal, echoed in the intuited voice of the little tree:

"You must let Michael go from you, Mary, from wanting him and looking for him. Do this for you as well as for him."

———

JIM AND I belonged to one of the small groups that had been meeting with Steve to share our imagery, and, if called for, to do more relevant journeying. Before we gathered the next day I spoke privately with Steve about my realization and concerns and proposed that I leave the group and join another one. He suggested that if I felt comfortable enough, I could share my reflections with Jim in the presence of the others.

"Bearing witness is part of your journey, a step along the path of your quest. This feels like an important piece of your healing and could be helpful for you and the group if you are willing to share it."

I did share in the presence of the others, despite the trembling that threatened to take over my body. As I spoke to Jim about Michael, I watched my twin fade from his persona. I noticed Jim's hair was a true brown. Mike's was sandy. Jim's face was more round than Michael's, his voice lower and his inflections more rapid and crisp. His gestures and the shape of his hands were entirely different from Michael's. He had a different stride. He didn't have the same laugh. How had I even thought he was like my twin?

I explained to Jim that, given my challenge, I felt we should try to stay focused on our connection to the group as a whole, that despite our private sharing, which I loved, it would be better for me now if we did not seek personal time together. Gratitude and warmth replaced my anxiety as he replied. He had listened with a quiet, open expression. He voiced his respect for my needs and my vision quest goal, and shared his own reasons for being drawn into a special relationship with me. He also felt caught in the past. Together, we honored the goodness of our friendship. The group voiced their gratitude, and many shared their own stories. I felt touched by all of them, becoming more open to and more accepting of myself again, and of my twisting, paradoxical path.

As we broke for lunch I lagged behind, a rising sadness seeping into the warmth of connection. Rather than the overwhelming, implosive tide that had threatened to drown me that first night, this was a quiet, naked resignation that opened to an underlying pool of deep feeling.

After lunch, I went back to my room and lay down. Sadness wrapped me like a blanket as I fell into dreamless sleep.

———

IN THE DAYS that followed at the lodge, we further explored and connected with the wisdom of our unconscious selves that emerged through our personal imagery journeys. According to Steve, our thinking mind is often critical and judgmental, and can separate us from other aspects of ourselves. In addition, the ways in which we connect with people socially do not usually lead us to getting to know all of who we are. Through forming relationships with the animal guides that appear in our imagery, we can discover and explore important parts of ourselves that are less familiar and even frightening. We can integrate them and find balance within. We can also connect with and heal places of injury, as well as appreciate positive attributes that have been unacknowledged, and therefore, have remained undeveloped. Steve had confidence that out of these interactive relationships, each of us would heal and grow.

In our next journey, we met imagery guides connected to four ways of understanding and relating to our world. Steve referred to them as the four windows of knowing: thinking, sensing, feeling, and imagery.

It is a gray, rainy morning. Water drops patter and slide down the windows of the meeting hall. As the group settles down, I close my eyes and call within for an animal from the window of thinking. A congested sensation occupies the space from my head to my chest. From within that space, an image of a hyena comes forth, his body dominated by a massive, square and ugly head. The hyena pants heavily and limps on three legs. One front paw is held in the air. He asks me to bandage the gash in his foot, which I do very gingerly with some gauze. I feel sorry for this animal and yet am repelled.

Steve asks us to request permission from our animal to merge with it so as to better understand its nature. The hyena agrees. I don't.

Steve's low voice seems to anticipate my reluctance, saying, "Just invite the merging and then allow whatever needs to happen."

I try to let go of my inhibition, and find myself mysteriously within the hyena, acutely aware of the power of his upper body, head, and huge jaw. I feel the weakness in his back legs, unbalancing him. The hyena shows me how he runs with his pack, collects others' garbage, and eats what the lions leave behind. He emits a high, silly laugh, which doesn't seem to match his body. He tells me he can't run with the pack anymore because of his wounded paw. He tells me he no longer fits in. I experience a strange sensation—an opening in the fur at the back of the hyena's and my neck. Spontaneously, I demerge and notice the wounded animal's dry, unkempt coat. He lies down, panting, his tongue lolling out of his mouth. I see another animal or something alive stirring within the growing split down his back. Earlier, I had felt the presence of a lioness nearby. Could that be the hidden animal? No, it doesn't seem to fit. Nothing more happens; the imagery fades. I am back in the big meeting room now, sensing the hyena is going to die and feeling incomplete.

Sunny, our family cat, emerges from the window of feeling. Fluffy, golden, and independent, he pees all over the house, making a smelly, annoying mess. As we merge, I feel him aloof—not needing to fit in. He wants to be let out of the house. I fear he might be killed or get Lyme disease or meet with a host of other problems; after all, he has no claws— he's a house cat. He does not respond to my concerns. Aware of his desire to be free, I reluctantly open the screen door and let him out. Sunny chews and rolls in the catnip growing by the well. He skids around the enclosed courtyard, coming to a stop in front of Oliver. High on the catnip, he bats Oliver in the nose with his clawless paw. Oliver, unperturbed, turns away, and Sunny stretches and lies on his back, biting and batting at dust particles floating in the sunlight. Understanding our house had become his cage, I realize it's better to be free than safe in a prison.

My window of sensing brings forth an ostrich. She has long legs, large feet, and a handsome array of dark, wide tail feathers. She does not look at me until I ask if I can do something for her. Shyly, she requests a pair of glasses so she can more easily relate to the world around her.

After I put a pair of glasses on her huge eyes, I feel the gentle touch of her head upon on my shoulder and sense her gratitude. I stroke her layered back feathers, soft and thick. Ostrich asks me to remove the stockings that cover her legs all the way up over her knobby, yellow knees. Merged, we stand, warm and comfortable in newly exposed skin. I recognize her ability to cover great distances, negotiating the terrain with her large, sensitive feet.

The animal appearing from the window of imagery is a mountain lion. She sits Sphinx-like on the ground. When I greet her and ask her what she has come to show me, she replies: "I am very powerful. It's who I am."

She asks me to take off her collar, which is unnecessary and too tight for her neck. As I do, her muscles swell, shift, and relax into place. We merge when I climb upon her back, running and leaping in the air with fully expressed power and freedom. Now off her back, we roll over and over in the grass, coming to rest as two separate beings in the full sun. The lioness raises her huge, graceful head and licks me. I am scrubbed clean by the gentle rasp of her tongue.

Now that we have met all our animals from the four modes of knowing, Steve asks us to invite them to meet together. Ostrich and Sunny the cat stay politely in their own worlds. Lion and Hyena walk solemnly together, with Hyena limping and falling behind. They lie down facing each other, nose to nose, their front paws touching.

Hyena has aged; he is totally gray. The split along his neck and back has widened, with pieces of fur hanging from its edges. Inside the split, an emerging form is not yet complete.

After lunch, Steve called our small group together. We shared our journeys, and then he asked if I wanted to talk to the new being and ask if it would like to come out. I agreed, feeling unfinished—the sense of being unbalanced had lingered.

I greet the hyena. He tells me he is dying and asks me to call forth the animal within its body. A young deer rises up from the split and steps gracefully out onto the ground. It wiggles its tail and stretches its legs, happy to have been born. I tell it I find it beautiful. The deer gazes at me with huge brown eyes and asks me to sit while it walks and gets used to its new surroundings.

My eyes finally turn from the deer to the hyena on the ground. He is dead. I am filled with tenderness.

———

THE LAST THREE days of our stay at the lodge were spent in direct preparation for the wilderness solo. I could feel our group energy intensifying and focusing as we reached for the tools to achieve our vision quest goals and meet the inner and outer challenges that lay ahead.

I felt as though pulled toward a long, dark tunnel carved out beneath the sea. Once inside, I knew there would be no way out except to keep moving forward, moving toward what I could not know, could not see, but desperately needed to trust. Bouts of anxiety controlled these nights. All my old safety concerns reared their heads. I had always been more cautious than Michael. By nature, he would happily strike out on a new path, while I would hold back. Yet in the end, Michael's free, engaged spirit had led to his death.

In the darkness of my small, bifurcated room, old, hollow, familiar voices whispered, barring the path to my solo. As I tossed and turned in bed, the chorus of voices pursued me, speaking first in one ear, then in the other of pending dangers. The voices eroded my vision of nature's connecting beauty, which I had experienced since my Medicine Walk. The wilderness ahead loomed as a place of territorial grizzlies, hidden spiders, chilling electrical storms, and even worse, a place where I might become hopelessly and irretrievably lost.

In the daylight the voices faded, replaced by images of my animals. From the crown of my head to the base of my spine they emerged, flooding my imagination, championing my path, and showing their support. I sensed the big elephant from my heart accompanied me on my afternoon walks. She lumbered along beside me, and when I stopped on the path and closed my eyes, I could feel my body lifted and gently rocked in the curve of her trunk. In those times, my heart swelled with gratitude and opened in fearless connection. And in the daylight I felt more bonded with my fellow questers, talking with them about our shared mission and the steps forward that we all needed to take.

Sam Jenkin brought my feelings of connection and support from the day and the emerging dread from the night together, when he suggested that we express our personal journeys in a drawing. He asked us to take a large piece of paper and draw images of our feelings about our impending solo and our vision quest goal.

"Don't think about how to do this exercise," he said. "Be spontaneous. Let your feelings express themselves directly through your pencils, and don't worry about whether you can draw; that's not the point. First, I want you to draw where you have come from—your state of mind when you arrived here."

I looked helplessly around the room, exchanging questioning, anxious looks with others in the group. Taking in a now-familiar deep breath and then letting it go, I waited for images to emerge. My crayon drew a huge cracked and gaping volcano. Fire and lava tears spewed from it into the sky and ran down its sides forming a vast sea, which engulfed the surrounding earth.

Sam then instructed us to draw our vision of where we would like to be. I drew the rose bush from my Medicine Walk. This time, it had just two roses on it, both in bloom and both hanging in separate places over the moving stream.

"What is the obstacle that keeps you from getting to where you want to be?" he asked.

The bat emerged. I drew it hanging from a branch, its wings fully open. Blood dripped from its gaping teeth. This image flowed unbidden from my pencil, frightening me. I started to cross it out and then stopped, remembering our task. *I'll never get there if I'm not true to myself,* I thought.

The bat stared at me from the page.

At the start of the exercise, we had been asked to crease our paper into quarters, folding over a quarter of the page as each drawing was finished. I did this now, hoping to blot out the bat's image and my fear with it.

One quarter of my page remained empty. Sam asked us to make a final drawing showing the way to overcome the obstacles to our goals. I closed my eyes feeling sudden tears. No answer or image came. Instead, I heard my own voice:

"Aren't you afraid when you dance under the moon that you might get eaten by an owl?"

"No, no, I'm not afraid," Rabbit replied. "I'm not afraid; I have the Dove of Peace."

I remembered the shadow of a dove that rested in the clouds above the crow's head—the crow that came from my crown chakra to tell me it will take what I am holding back of Michael up to the heavens when I am ready to let it go. Choosing a gray outline pencil and a white crayon, I drew a dove in the remaining space. It came out very small, a tiny, rounded bird, wings closed but suspended within a vast expanse of sky.

As we unfolded our papers, I saw the path of my journey spread before me. I was struck by the stark difference between the images of the problem and the images of the solution; the polarity between the destroying images of the volcano of fiery, drowning tears, and the bloody-mouthed bat; versus the delicate, vulnerable, yet fearless and peaceful images of the tiny dove in an endless sky and the two separate roses suspended above a flowing stream. I regarded these powerful images without any sense of how to move forward. My legs felt tired, though I was sitting on my mat. The next step seemed out of reach.

STEVE GALLEGOS STOPPED me in the hallway after lunch, asking if I would be willing to forgo my walk and meet with our small group one last time in preparation for the solo. I readily agreed. We gathered in a separate sitting area off the dining room. Steve asked us to sit, and to silently offer our support and presence as he guided each of us on a separate journey. When it was my turn, I showed him my drawing, explaining my fearful reaction to the bat.

"I think I have to talk to it," I said, "although I don't really want to." I gave a nervous laugh.

Steve remained serious. "Let your animals decide who wants to talk to you."

Again I confronted my reluctance to let go and allow my inner wisdom to present itself as it saw fit.

It is Sunny, my cat, who comes now, the animal guide from the window of feeling. He rolls in the catnip by the well at my home. He wants me to join him, so we lie among the tiny, purple-flowered stems and play. He punches me with his soft paws; I tickle his tummy. He bites my hand gently. We're the same size. Sunny rises from the now matted-down catnip and walks purposefully out of the courtyard into the garden. I follow. At the same moment I realize he is on a hunt, he appears by my side with a chipmunk in his mouth.

"Let it go! Stop killing. Why do you do that?"

"It is what I do. It is what I am meant to do for my life."

He shakes the chipmunk, breaking its neck, and drops it at my feet, running off. I stare at the lifeless little body. A rush of feeling brings tears as I realize I cannot stop death. I weep and weep, until I sense another self, standing, silently observing me. I tell Steve this and he gently asks me to greet this self and ask her what she comes to show me. She explains that she is the one who brings the numbing fog, which hasn't allowed me to feel. I ask her if she would only watch from now on and not get in the way of my feelings. She agrees and fades. A vast, limitless place of feeling surrounds and holds me. I am at peace.

CHAPTER TWENTY-ONE

_____

RESTING IN MY ROOM after the journey with Steve, I became acutely aware that we would be leaving the following morning for the wilderness experience, and more important, for the solo. I had no more thoughts of backing out. I had entered the tunnel. I was not able to see the light at the end, but I was no longer alone. The wisdom and strength of my animals and their loving presence was mine if I chose to embrace it. I was still supported by the peaceful feeling that had enveloped me when I turned away from the figure of numbness.

———

THERE WERE TO be two ceremonies that final evening—a tonal dance and an indigenous ritual of purification called a sweat lodge. Both were to take place outside after dark. From my reading about tonal dance, I knew it was a vehicle for spiritual communication and transformation. The participant dances in order to animate his or her quest and empower it to manifest. Each dancer's dress expresses the spirit of his or her personal journey, and each person dances as that spirit, honoring his or her animal guides.

The dance is also an opportunity to engage and tame the fears and insecurities that shadow the quester. Recently, Sam Jenkin had seemed to be aloof. His manner in relating to me felt impersonal, even a bit cold. I wondered if it was the result of something I had done. Privately, I had spoken to him about my feelings and my desire to get my reaction to him into perspective so it would not inhibit my goals. I had told him I wanted to break my pattern of needing to develop twinlike intimacy with men, and described what had happened with Jim. Sam proposed we explore this dynamic in ceremony, and suggested I approach him during the tonal dance. He had grinned, adding he might or might not accept my invitation to dance, as he'd recently become Coyote, the Native American trickster. "Lighten up, Mary," he seemed to be saying. "Keep your sense of humor." This talk about becoming Coyote seemed a bit weird, coming from a psychologist, but then, so much of what I had been experiencing during the last week felt outside of my world of expectations and I knew Sam was helping me. I decided to try to relax and trust his approach.

In preparation for the second ceremony, all the questers had participated in the building of a sweat lodge, a hut-like structure made of pine boughs and formed into a circle around a fire pit. On the eve of the solo, chants and prayers are offered by the participants while sweating out physical impurities in the high temperature generated by fire-heated rocks, which are rolled into the pit. Later, prayers of gratitude and supplication are also offered on behalf of all the questers, their loved ones, and the "Returning to Earth" community.

Intense heat, which I had previously found seriously enervating, frightened me. In addition, we were told that it is both traditional and healthier to enter the sweat lodge naked, so that our bodies could perspire freely. Although it was to be a personal choice, we were encouraged to do so. The thought of joining our male and female group naked felt uncomfortably self-exposing. I discussed the idea with several apprehensive women in our group. We agreed to wait until the moment of the ceremony to decide how far we would undress and whether we would stay in the heat.

In the late afternoon, I began my preparations for the tonal dance. I had chosen the beech leaf from my Medicine Walk as the symbol of my quest and now of my dance. It lay intact in its small box, one side crumpled and brown, the other a vibrant yellow. A tiny brown stain encroached into the yellow glow from the dead half. I placed the leaf in an open book where I could easily see it, and with watercolors and a mirror painted my face—the left side dusty brown with dark lines for the leaf folds, the right side lemon yellow. I wore a long-sleeved white Mexican Indian dress. Under the skirt, I put on woolen underwear to resemble Native American leggings. My prized Cree Indian wedding moccasins finished the look; their soft, beaded deerskin molded to my feet and laced to the calf. My body was completely covered except for my hands. They looked naked and out of place. Painting the left one brown and the right one yellow to match my face, I remembered that I use my left hand and Michael his right. From deep within came the fleeting thought: *It is me who is dying now, not Michael.*

There is no rising moon this evening as I walk to the dance. Warm night air and a clear starry sky welcome me into the encroaching darkness. I am anxious about what is to come, but I trust the guides and feel close to the other questers who walk with me now, each in their special symbolic costumes, each of us entering into experiences we have never had.

As we arrive at the hilltop, our four guides hand us rattles and small drums and motion us to form a circle. Ann starts a slow, rhythmic beat with her drum and begins to move. The other guides follow her lead, nodding to us to join in. I move easily, echoing the drumbeat with my rattle and my feet. I respond to the simple, tonal rhythm in an old language, a language I know in some ancient part of myself, one that flows from me now, thrilled to be given expression. I am the half-dead beech leaf. I come into being in the movement of my feet. I dance with a life force that circles and flows outward, spreading through my swaying arm and opening yellow hand— then shrinking and folding inward in a death grip as my brown hand and face turn down toward the center of the circle. Opening and closing, I become the sound; I become the rhythm; I become the cry for my vision.

With her deep, penetrating drum, Ann calls to me. I wake, as if from a trance, to see others dancing in relationship. Ann approaches me with the languid movements of a cat. Unbidden, my mountain lion leaps to my side. We merge; my body springs into lithe motion. I brush against Ann, purring and growling. As two powerful cats, we circle each other in play. We circle and sway, carried by the movement and sound until our play knows its rightful ending and we effortlessly rejoin the circle.

Sam stands alone at the periphery. I gesture for him to come into the circle. He looks directly at me and quickly moves out of sight, melting into the darkness. His sudden disappearance is jarring, but I breathe in the lively mood of the dancers and keep moving. Abruptly, Sam enters the circle in front of me and turns to face me, jumping in double time at my feet. We laugh and shake our rattles, teasing each other, coming together and pulling away, twirling faster and faster. As I come out of a twirl, he is gone. I hesitate. My mood lifts with delight.

Questers come in and out of my orbit, welcoming, connecting, and then releasing. All of life breathes in and out, held in the safe tonal rhythms and nourished within the circle.

———

The night has darkened. We move from the tonal dance to the ceremony of the sweat lodge; the closed, hot dwelling looms claustrophobic. In a sudden, desperate effort to stay connected, I remove my clothes and enter the lodge naked.

To hell with everything! If I'm going to do this, I might as well do it all the way.

I find a seat next to Agnes, another woman scared of the rising temperature. We are close to the entrance and can both leave without disrupting the group. Hot rocks are rolled into the pit, each rock intensifying the heat in the dark, crowded space. Agnes and I whisper. In trying to calm her, I reassure myself.

As leader, Ann offers prayers of respect to the earth and the sky. Following her lead, we pray spontaneously out loud, our voices hesitant at first and then stronger, overlapping and filling the sweat lodge with sound. The growing pile of heat-soaked rocks glows red in the pit, radiating more intensely. My body pours sweat, which runs down my face and torso in rivulets. My skin prickles ominously. The air closes in upon me, full to bursting with voices, closely packed bodies, and smothering heat. Without warning, Agnes leaves. I panic, ready to follow, but Sam's voice rises within me, reminding me to breathe in and roar when the heat feels too much. No one else is leaving.

Raising a desperate prayer for my survival, I take in a breath and let it out in a harsh-sounding croak. I breathe in again. I become Mountain Lion and roar. I roar again and again, drawing upon the strength of her great, feline body. My heart settles. My voice carries my prayers. The thick, entreaty-filled darkness becomes a mysterious vessel into which I pour my supplication. I pray for help; I pray for a vision to guide me; I pray for a vision to free me so I might free Michael, so I might let him go.

The voices and the ubiquitous sweat and the unseen nakedness and the tiny closeted space bring me to my grounding snake with her eggs and to the egg with me inside its shell. All around me—one group, one nest. We each move within the rhythm of our own breath, dancing our own dance, encased within our own shells—all stretching, all crying to be reborn.

Upon completion of the ceremony, we crawled out of the sweat lodge and lay exhausted and naked around the fire. Ann came out and stretched on the ground next to me. I put my arm under her head. Our sweat dried, leaving us cool. We rose and walked among the naked male and female forms to our dressing places and put on our clothes. No one noticed, no one spoke. Each had turned inward, exploring his or her own space. I felt cleansed and beautifully safe.

Back at the lodge, I slept deeply without a dream. When I awoke to the new day, my sensitive, self-irritated, fearful, contracting self did not accompany me. I felt open and free to wonder.

CHAPTER TWENTY-TWO

THE FIRST MORNING OF our wilderness experience had begun. That morning, all fifteen questers, accompanied once again by our oversized backpacks, and Ann and Jeanne (our new outdoor guide), set out by bus for a prearranged meeting place. There we relinquished our heavy gear to three jeeps. We were to meet up with the gear later near the trailhead that led to our base camp. In the meantime, we would spend our day walking in silent meditation and reflection toward our wilderness destination. We followed a gradual, ascending trail, a gentle, pleasant hike. I was vividly aware of the companionship of my animals. We moved together to an inner marching song, lifting me forward toward my solo. The morning sunlight, whispering grasses, and shadowed woodland glades bordering the path reinforced my sense of place.

Released from my isolation surrounding Michael's death, I experienced a lightness of body and being. In our group discussions of the past week, nothing impelled me to excuse my loneliness or explain away the shame and fear that characterized the enormous power that Michael's death held over me. Nor did I need to excuse the giant, emotional step I had taken in releasing my denial and grief that first evening. Within our group, no one questioned the legitimacy of anyone else's feelings. My reality remained consistently respected and supported. As a result, I was increasingly able to respect and support myself and my goals for the quest.

No longer threatened by the nightmarish fears of abandonment and survival I had imagined experiencing during the four days and three nights of the solo, I walked with new resolve along the sunny trail. What had happened to me? Perhaps those fears had helped to disguise the core fear that overtook me that first night of the quest: *Michael is dead, and like him, I will drown.* But I did not drown, and throughout the next seven days what had been hidden was exposed, freeing me to find new strengths and new perspectives.

I thought of my experience with Jim, to whom I had been drawn into an immediate sense of intimate relationship, of the stark moment when I realized I had made him my twin, and of the genuine warmth I felt for him and for myself as I released the bonds of this illusion. Seeing him for who he really was, just present for me as a friend, brought a new comfort in myself as separate.

Thinking back to the sweat lodge, I smiled, thrilled and grateful I had found the guts to strip off my clothes and step in and breathe in that fiery air, melting and shedding years of encrusted, ingrown doubt and fear, finding in my nakedness my true cry to let Michael go, my cry to be born anew.

On the trail, in those first few miles of our walk to the wilderness camp all of nature supported a sense of connection, and the silence and rhythm of my feet opened me to the sweetness of the new home I was going to meet.

———

The group ahead slowed, and the woman directly in front of me stopped on the trail, waking me from my reverie.

"I think we're lost," she whispered. "I heard Ann say that we're not where we should be on her map of the trail."

We moved into a huddle with two other women who had stopped nearby. Whispers of concern spread down the line of questers. Spontaneously, we dropped the agreed-upon silence and broke into open discussion. Jeanne, our new guide, made the decision to branch off onto the left fork ahead. Our trail ascended for about two more miles, until it abruptly ended with a view overlooking an undulating sweep of open land. The higher foothills spread out in the near distance, behind them the peaks of the San Juan Mountains. Before us, a disintegrating post-and-rail fence surrounded a large overgrown field, three ancient log cabins, and a now roofless, rectangular barn. Other than our trail, there was no entrance to this compound. I wondered how anyone could have farmed in this exquisite, inaccessible place.

Everyone expressed an opinion; in the face of our apparent dilemma, Jeanne no longer commanded the group. The other leaders, Sam, Mel, and Steve, were not present. Sam, an experienced hiker and wilderness guide familiar with the area, was to join us somewhere along the path. It wasn't clear exactly where that would be.

Ann finally spoke up. "We'd better retrace our steps," she said. "Sam will realize we are lost and will wait for us. We'll find him once we rejoin the original trail."

I was worried. I didn't understand how he would know where to wait, but no other practical plan presented itself. A grumble rose from the ranks of questers. My lightweight daypack suddenly weighed heavily on me. Back on the trail, my feet plodded along, having forgotten their rhythm. I kept the pace with considerable effort. Behind me, my roommate Alice lagged, slowing her stride and the group behind her. I called ahead a few times to get the leaders to stop while she rested. Finally, I sped up to tell Ann that Alice needed help. We stopped again while Ann went back to reassure and encourage her. After what seemed like hours, we found Sam. He showed us where we had missed the trail, a hidden place where the path had branched off under a fence.

From the moment Sam arrived, the atmosphere changed. There was no stopping now, no more catering to our fatigue. We began a steep ascent. Silence resumed. We stopped to drink and rest when the trail finally broke from the woods, opening again onto a field. Like tipped dominos, we fell one after another to the ground. Although vivid peaks thrust skyward in jagged splendor around us, no one seemed to notice them.

"It's easy from here on," Sam said, answering a quester's worried question. "It's all downhill."

For me this "easy" downhill trail was the most difficult leg of our journey—eight hundred feet straight down a slippery, winding, gravel-strewn path. Twice I fell on my butt, once nearly sliding into the steep ravine that dropped off from the right side of the trail. My knees were killing me by the time we reached the narrow valley floor and the three waiting jeeps. Accompanied by the now irritatingly enthusiastic and directive voice of Sam, I struggled to lift and get into the shoulder harness of my heavy pack. I had never walked any distance with it before. Besides its weight, the top-heavy load was difficult to balance.

The mile-long trail ahead lay flat until the last hundred yards, when it ascended to the top of a hill. Here it ended at our campsite. That last climb created more physical distress than I had ever experienced. Every part of my body hurt. As we started up the final incline, my legs were shaking. I had trouble catching my breath. Tears of defeat filled my eyes. I gasped to Peter, the large, gentle quester behind me, that I could not go another step.

"I know you feel it's impossible, Mary, but you can," he answered. "I'll show you; just stay next to me."

Peter let the other questers pass us while I leaned against a tree.

Then, with his calm, reassuring voice, he taught me how to breathe, how to walk, and how to rest. With a strong and generous spirit, he talked me through each slow, ascending step until we reached our campsite.

———

THE FIRST TWO nights of our outdoor experience and the day in between were spent in final preparation for our four-day solos: choosing the campsite for our respective sites—our personal "power spot"—reviewing logistical plans, learning camping skills, and receiving further psychological preparation for the separation from our group. This preparatory time was to be a silent period, except when we were being helped or instructed by a guide or another quester or were engaged in an interactive group session.

The base camp spread out over the surface of the hilltop, our tarps and sleeping bags making a random pattern among a thin stand of deciduous trees and pines. We found an old fire pit in a centrally located clearing, which we lined with stones and used for cooking. Numerous flat-topped rocks left by former campers formed a larger circle surrounding the pit. These we used as seats when we gathered to eat or to meet as a group.

I spent the first night under my flat, rectangular, nylon tarp, which was suspended off the ground between two trees by a horizontal rope and held open by four ropes staked to the earthen floor. After I climbed into my sleeping bag, I noticed that the ground beneath the tarp slanted, causing my body to list and feel off balance. I discovered that my down sleeping bag was not warm enough to keep out the July mountain cold. As I turned and twisted to get comfortable, one of the male questers nearby began to snore. The snores grew into intermittent bursts of pig-like snuffles and grunts, impossible to ignore. After the long hike, our meal had been light, in preparation for the days of fasting ahead. I was hungry. My stomach growled.

My knees and back ached, and the slanting ground felt lumpy and unforgivingly hard. I thought of getting out of my sleeping bag and trying to find more clothes from my pack, but rejected the idea; I didn't want to wake the others. Besides, I couldn't remember where I had put my flashlight. Instead, I shivered, tossed, and worried.

Ten years earlier my thyroid had been removed, making it difficult for me to control the temperature of my body. Because of this, I had decided to pack a small pup tent in case it rained, but had given up the idea of using it when I realized no one else had brought one. Now I didn't care. *What if it goes below freezing*, I thought, *and I get hypothermia on my solo? I'm not Sam. Tomorrow I'm using my tent!* My worries continued. *Shit*, I thought—*with no thyroid, what if fasting is bad for my body? Why didn't I think to ask the doctor before I left?*

I stewed in this dilemma, until I remembered with relief the four little bags of trail mix I had guiltily stuffed in my pack at home before I left. *So, good for me! I'm going on my solo, aren't I*—I took a deep breath—*I'm* not *backing out.*

Prior remarks of a few members of our group crowded into my mind. They had been talking about walking up to five miles from camp to find their sites so they would be sure to have privacy. *No way*, I thought. *I'm not going farther than one-half mile from this hill!* I closed my eyes and took another deep breath—*no, don't go there, Mary. I am* not *backing out.*

Worry cascaded over worry; it was dawn before I fell into an exhausted sleep.

———

The next morning after a breakfast of miso soup and a piece of fruit, we set out to find our power spots. Pushing away the concerns of the previous night, I tried to focus on the idea the guides had shared with us that this place of power we sought was a place that would bring our inner and outer worlds together.

There were many spots to choose from. The land spread out at the bottom of our hill, forming a grass-covered valley dotted with pines, and was bordered on one side by a broad stream, which sourced from high up in the steep rock shelves of a mountainous ravine. Once the stream emerged from the woods, it ran gently downhill through open fields and disappeared from view behind the lower mounds of the San Juan foothills. These hills folded and spread southward, interrupted by outcroppings of rock and woodlands.

Morning sun filled the valley floor with the smell of pine sap and delicate wild flowers in full bloom. I was surrounded by bird song and the buzz and whining hum of insects. The unmet challenges and fears of the night before evaporated as I breathed in the warm, evocative air and took in the clear beauty of the day.

All the questers and Steve Gallegos, the only staff member who had chosen to go on a solo, walked together down the hill to the valley floor and then split off into small groups, headed in the directions to which they were drawn. We were encouraged to be spontaneous in our decision-making, much like on the Medicine Walk. I found myself immediately drawn to the stream. About six of us walked toward it across the field and then four split off, heading northward on the mountain trail that led up the ravine. That left Steve and me. We laughed about how we both wanted to stay near the base camp. We agreed then to be buddies. As required by vision quest protocol, this meant we'd be responsible for each other's safety during our solos. We would only see each other if there were an emergency, but would check on each other's well-being at separate appointed times and at an agreed-upon site. There we would each place a special stone upon a log signaling to the other that we were fine. If we didn't find our buddy's sign, we would know something was amiss and would go to the other's camp to offer help and make contact with the base camp if necessary.

Steve and I separated after making these plans. He walked northwest through the high grass, and I headed upstream where the field merged with trees. My power spot presented itself within five minutes of leaving him. A deer path, bordering the creek, had beckoned to me and I had followed it, watching the fields disappear and the bushes and the forest present themselves. On my right, in the middle of a large stand of towering pines, a glen opened up. It was situated about seventy feet in from the stream, and had a narrow view of the water. There, the forest floor gently rose up from the stream bed and lay covered in clumps of maidenhair fern and various kinds of moss and pine cones. In the sunnier spots, cream and purple columbine grew, and other wildflowers I didn't recognize. The enormous pines bordered the glen and continued down to the bank of the now-rushing stream. Their great limbs emerged from wide columnar trunks and stretched out twenty feet or more above the ground. I walked back to the stream, aware of its voice defining the whole space with continuous, unfolding sound. As I reached its edge, a large doe bolted from the deep woods on the other side and disappeared behind a rock outcropping. Could this be a vision of my thinking animal now fully grown?

Behind the glen, and about one hundred feet in from the stream, I found an area where a slow brook and marshland deepened into a tiny pond. It reminded me of Michael and New Guinea, the way the land and the water intertwined when they met. The clearing in the woods and the large stream evoked memories of Maine and Wyoming, places that Michael and I both visited as we grew up. I kept wandering from one exquisite site to the next. Just in from the edge of the clearing, and looking north through the upper branches of a stand of deciduous trees, I discovered a round opening, a leaf-framed view of three radiant mountain peaks, each emitting a mysterious, pink glow. I held my breath imagining I had accidentally come upon an ancient triptych, a luminous, majestic masterpiece suspended above the altar of a hidden chapel—a sacred site, which infused my body in a halolike shimmer. In that radiant immediacy I knew I had found my power spot.

The whole site opened like an idyllic dream, an exquisite, consecrated creation filled with the best of nature's offerings. I vowed to embrace the gifts of this sacred place, to grow beyond the boundaries of my fears, to enter nature's heart and bear witness to Michael's life and death, and to find the courage to let him go.

STEVE AND I reconnected at our checking-in place. We took each other to our respective power spots before making our way back to base camp. It was late afternoon by the time we reached the top of the hill. The rest of the day was spent around the fire pit discussing last-minute questions and concerns. Mel Bucholtz, our third leader, seemed to read my mind when he brought up the subject of fear.

"Our inner fear," he told us, "is a natural part of the quest for and process of major change. Recognize the power you are making claim to in seeking the goal of your vision quest. The fear you meet is a measure of this power. Fear can be your teacher now. It can organize and focus your attention and your challenge. Ask it what it has to teach you. The more you do this, the more fear will loosen its hold on you. Fear, like pain, feeds on your not accepting it. If you push it away, it can grow, even make you feel crazy, which believe me, you are not. As you move toward and into relationship with fear, you will achieve equal status with what frightens you. Fear can become your ally."

Mel's wise words opened up the subject for all of us. As I listened to others and shared my own thoughts and feelings, I felt less alone with my fear. Sam stressed getting into relationship with our bodies when we felt scared. He offered us a process:

"First, sit holding your knees, or stand, feeling the support of your body connected to the ground. You can also make contact with a tree or a large rock, which will help you to ground yourself. Now scan your body, listen within, and locate which part of your body holds the fear." Steve continued, inviting us to call for our animal guide from the energy center nearest that part of the body.

"Ask your animal if it needs anything from you, and if it will stay with you."

Finally, Sam reiterated Mel's words: "Ask the fear what it wants."

Mel broke in, "And above all, keep your sense of humor. Tell it, 'Oh, there you are, fear. I can tell you want something from me.' If fear wants to, let it devour you. Believe me, it will get a stomachache and spit you out—reborn."

We all laughed.

———

AS I LAY in my sleeping bag that night I thought about the time we had spent at the lodge, talking about our realistic and practical fears about camping alone in nature, such as what to do you if you met a bear or a skunk or were in a lightning storm. The more amorphous fears we shared around the fire seemed to arise from within. I saw how I projected these concerns onto the outside world—they grew into fears of large hairy bugs, angry grizzlies, and raging storms, everything blown out of proportion. How paradoxical and hopeful to think of fear as a teacher—as an energy that might even propel me forward on my path.

———

WITH A NEW location and the extra layer of insulation provided by my tent, my body was warm and relatively comfortable in my sleeping bag. I awoke in the middle of the night to a full moon. The damp night air encouraged my need to pee. When I crawled back into my sleeping bag, I felt a wave of nausea and noticed that my stomach hurt. Part of me watched as anxiety crept in, growing into a feeling of alarm. *What if I am getting sick? What then? How will I ever . . .*

Worries gathered momentum. Thoroughly uncomfortable, I sat up with my legs bent as Sam had advised. My head touched the top of the tent. My hands found my sore stomach. I focused on my breath, breathing in the earth beneath me, feeling its support. I greeted the pain and my sense of alarm. I was about to invite the animal from my belly chakra, the place where I was the most uncomfortable, when I remembered I'd had a dream:

I am going somewhere. I try to leave the house but the door won't close behind me. It doesn't fit the opening. I leave the house with the door open. Approaching the new place, I realize I've left behind my suitcase with all my clothes. It's too late to go back. I will have to improvise. I'm not that upset. I feel I have to get a key from someone to do something for myself and then the others. Finally, I get the key from some men. I run around the house to the front door.

One man shouts after me, "You'll see. That's not the key; it won't open the door."

Now I am going somewhere in a taxi. The driver takes me to the wrong address. Things are not working out the way I planned, but I am not upset or scared.

The dream left everything unresolved, but somehow in remembering it, it felt complete and I was not afraid—my anxiety had disappeared. I warmed my stomach with my hands. Perhaps the ache and nausea were a simple reaction to the greatly restricted diet we'd had the previous two days. Turning on my stomach, I gazed out the open flap of the tent at the moonlit trees.

May I have the courage to allow a knowing bigger than my fearful mind.

CHAPTER TWENTY-THREE

VISION QUEST SOLO JOURNAL

IT IS THE first day of my solo. I write this journal from my power spot, sitting against a rock near the stream.

After an early-morning severance ceremony at base camp, everyone hugged one another goodbye. I shed a few tears. Steve and I met at the crown of the hill. He helped me on with my pack, and we set out to our meeting place halfway between our two power spots. We briefly reviewed our checking-in process: which stones we would place on the log to show the other we were safe and what times of the day we would go to the log so as to avoid meeting each other. We stood awkwardly with our top-heavy packs and water bags dangling from the bottom straps. Steve laughed when I leaned against a tree, understanding from my expression that I was drawn to sit down before I even got started. We wished each other well. We couldn't hug—too much paraphernalia in between. It was very sweet.

Ann had given me a citrine stone and asked that I bury it for Michael. Yesterday she and I discussed the form my solo would take—she made notes as I voiced my ideas. I love my sister. She has been wonderfully supportive to me during this whole process, and a generous and effective leader, offering creative support to many people. I was touched by her remarks as well as those of several of the other questers. Their warm feelings made me realize again how happy I am when I move away from the judgment of myself and others. What a waste.

When I entered my power spot, I sensed that this magical enclave had been waiting for me. I set up my tent and tarp at the far end of the glen. Warm, fragrant air wafted through the enclosed space as I unpacked. When I straightened up, and turned toward the stream, I found a young buck staring at me. He stood, muzzle dripping, in the middle of the rushing water. Honoring his domain, I bowed slightly in greeting and sat down out of view, hoping if I was quiet he would stay. When I rose again, he had vanished—no sound, not even when he left the stream.

FIRST DAY—2 P.M.—IN MY TENT

Putting up the tarp and tent took a lot of energy. I feel quite weak. I have eaten one of the four small packets of dried fruit and nuts and am drinking lots of water. The two water bags felt like rocks when I hoisted and tied them to a tree. A while ago, I walked upstream and found a beautiful place for Michael's burial service. An old hollow tree stump not far from the water will be the burial site. Exploring further, a pouring, gushing sound led me to an exquisite waterfall, and at its base a series of small rapids—another gift.

I'm very tired. It feels like rain. Where's my flashlight? Just as I settle into my tent, I keep forgetting things I left outside and have to get up again. Chipmunks are squeaking, probably having a fit with an intruder so close to their home. I found an especially private place to pee and an-other place to poop—not bad. Am burying my waste and my toilet paper.

Have time to rest for two hours until four p.m., when I'll get the other water bags from the rock pile at our meeting place. Afterward, the dedication ceremony, and then to bed before dark.

FIRST DAY—5 P.M.

The two water bags were right where I'd left them. I hope Steve finds the stone I left on the log.

How should I shape my solo? I need to honor Mike's life, honor our life together, give him the funeral I was not present for. I had told Ann that I didn't remember Mike's church service or the placing of his memorial stone in the family burial plot. We both agreed now would be the perfect time to have my own memorial service. It's huge—I have never laid him to rest.

Ann had reminded me of the vision quest solo goals when we talked together: the quester dies to the life stage that is finished in order to be present for his or her new path. What does this mean for me? My goal is to let Michael go. I told her I was confused and concerned about how to make this happen. She said one way would be to follow my intuition and let the process unfold spontaneously in ceremony.

FIRST DAY—8 P.M.—IN MY TENT

I set up a circle of stones, which I declare a sacred, ceremonial space. Here I will pray for the inner power to achieve my goals. All the tools I will need for the ceremonies are waiting for me here in this glen.

I feel compelled to write down the form for my time here—to make a structure within which I can move in spontaneity, but that will motivate me when I am afraid and help guide me to receive the gifts of this sacred place. I think I know now what shape some of it will take:

Dedication Ceremony

Preparation of burial site—tomorrow at the stump

Memorial—bearing witness to Mike—marsh

Funeral service—stump

Letting Michael go—how to? Don't yet know

Rebirth!?

DEDICATION CEREMONY

I kneel in the circle of stones and place one of Michael's letters in the center and one in my shirt next to my heart.

I give thanks to nature—the forest, the stream, and the plants—for allowing me to make this my power spot. I thank the sky, the earth, and my animals for their support and ask all to help me in my quest. Out loud, I state that my solo is dedicated to Michael and me and our twinship. I ask God, the Great Mystery, to bless us in saying goodbye to each other. I speak to Mike. I tell him I want to exchange gifts with him, so that each of us might benefit from the other's strengths, so we might support each other on our separate paths. I pray for support for our rebirths.

To Michael, I give my good judgment and a clear sense of reality. I ask for his ability to joyfully embrace life without hesitation and without fear. I tell Mike I want to give him a real funeral, one of the earth and of the spirit that connects things and connects us, too. I want to honor him and our twinship and then to let him go so that he might be free to travel on whatever his new path is, and I might be free to grow in the places where I haven't yet been able to without him. I pray we will both be reborn, always loving each other, but that I can be free of mourning him and looking for him in other relationships.

A LIGHT PATTER of rain on the tent; thunder growls in the distance. The darkening sky barely shows between the clouds. The stream splashes and rushes away outside the glen. Suddenly, I feel separate—alone—*if only Oliver was here with me*. I pray to my imagery animals to protect me, to the big trees to imbue me with their strength, and to Mother Earth to be my bed.

Dear Elephant! Her trunk slides beneath my body, lifting me—rocking me back and forth . . .

SECOND DAY—DAWN—IN MY TENT

Dreams from the night before—trying to disappear:

I dream I am having a dream in which I had a stroke. I cannot talk and am struggling to speak. I wake within the dream calling Tom's name. I am sleeping next to him again—so cozy and safe. His big arms hold me. I don't understand why we split.

Tom is dressed in an Arab outfit. We are somewhere in Baghdad; he was on assignment. I follow him into a mosque where there is a service only for men. Tom disappears. I cannot find him in the outer room. Women are not allowed in the main room. It is dark and smoky.

Then I am in a hotel and lose my wallet. I have no money, no identification. I keep wandering and looking at things I want to bring home as souvenirs of the journey.

I wake up remembering Tom. I don't miss him—it must be Michael I was dreaming of! Another fragment: *I am wearing strange clothes.*

Through one of the outfits, you can see my body. I explain to the people around me that where I had been I was used to being naked—that's what we did there.

Sleep comes again—no further dreams.

SECOND DAY—11 A.M.

Last night I slept on and off for twelve hours. It's a miracle that I didn't need to go to the bathroom, even though I awoke at night. There were no real animals close by; at least, if there were any, they were quiet.

I emerged from my tent at 9 a.m. and prepared for the day. The flies and mosquitoes appeared at 10. Where was yesterday's breeze? The bugs make it necessary for me to wear a scarf plus my baseball cap under the hood of my rain poncho. Otherwise, bug spray or no bug spray, I can't write—unless, of course, I zip myself into my tent. When I have my gloves on, my face is the only available meal. Every time the whining comes near, I blow mightily—about every fifteen seconds.

It is amazing how I have adapted: putting up my tarp and tent, sleeping on the ground, sitting on the ground, my water procedures, washing procedures, eliminating procedures, making tea on the Sterno. I am not even that hungry—still haven't figured out how to hold my metal cup over the Sterno without getting burned. I use a forked stick, but by the time the tea gets hot, the cup is boiling to the touch, and the stick is on fire. If I wait until the cup's cool enough to touch, the tea is no longer hot—I'll never be Jane, forget Tarzan. Next time, if there is one, I'll bring a pot and a stove mitt.

I know I should plan Mike's funeral service. I keep putting it off. Thunder sounds again, despite the clear day. It is easy to just gaze through my tree window at the mountaintops.

SECOND DAY—EVENING, 8 P.M. IN MY TENT

What a delicate, overwhelming day—so difficult for me to start and then it just unfolded and fell into place. My body feels as if it's trying to catch up. It's hypersensitive and vulnerable—especially my skin and my heart.

I am not lonely or afraid—it feels right to be here alone. It's not a time for another person—not a time to talk—yet I need to write down what has happened, so I will never forget.

This morning it was my turn to go to the stone pile—something to do, to put off what I could not start. When I came back, I stood in the circle of stones. I told my imagery animals I did not want to begin, even though I knew I was ready. Deep inside, they gathered quietly and stood silent—waiting. I wept. Afterward, I started—just like that, like I was very simply released.

PREPARATION OF THE BURIAL SITE

I walk to the gravesite I have chosen for Michael's burial ceremony and spend the rest of the morning in preparation there. The old stump sits within a small ring of huge columnar pines, a continuation of the grove that grows in and around my sleeping and ceremonial glen. It is as if this circular opening is a sacred side room in my forest home. Through a break in the circle of pines, a group of aspen trees enters the space. At their roots lie two decaying logs, which point the way to the center of the stump. Their papery silver bark separates from their decaying inner cores. Groups of tiny new pines and moss grow out of this dying-living soil, and various types of shelflike fungi cling to the bark.

Like a giant in a fairy glen, I carefully look for a place to sit near the stump so as not to disturb the meandering groups of toadstools, each with its smooth, shiny, bronze top. They seem to grow before my eyes, pushing aside the pine needles that lie between clumps of moss, bunchberries, and star-like, white flowers. A few noiseless insects are drawn to these flowers. I imagine the tiny drops of nectar held for them in the centers of the petals. The stream is about fifteen feet away. It bubbles and gurgles and smoothes out—a happy, releasing sound.

The old stump is almost covered with a thin layer of moss. Its sides have nearly worn away, leaving one encircling arm of wood and a deep indentation in the middle where the trunk has rotted to form a soft, rusty red floor—perfect for a burial.

As markers for Michael's grave, I find two pieces of pine bark to represent ceremonial shields from the Asmat. On one, I carve a pattern of cowry shells, the Asmat's most precious ceremonial adornment. On the other, I carve a simple Asmat design of a praying mantis, a powerful symbol of death and rebirth. I find a small branch from a deciduous tree. This I break in two, keeping the piece that is straight and which includes a tiny horizontal arm sticking out close to the top. This piece of wood will represent a bis pole, one of the seven totem poles Mike collected from the Asmat. These magnificent 15- to 30-foot poles are the centerpieces of the Asmat ceremony and feast that is held to commemorate and release the spirits of their dead. Asmat people consider themselves to be people of the tree. The bis pole is made from the trunk of a mangrove tree, carved with the figures of ancestors and often a canoe to symbolize the spiritual journey of liberation. At its top is a protruding lattice-designed *cemen*, or phallus, which symbolizes fertility and new life. The bis poles are also carved as a reminder that the spirits of important Asmat ancestors must be revenged to be released, hence the connection of this ceremony to the practice of headhunting. The head of the person killed in revenge symbolizes the fruit of new life, much as fruit with its seeds carries on the life of a tree. For Mike's burial, I will place my bis pole on his grave, symbolizing his death and rebirth. I want the energy from this symbolic pole to help me release what I hold back of Michael's presence, so he will be completely freed for his new life.

I lay the two shields and the bis pole next to each other, and gently remove the rich red soil from the center of the stump in preparation for the burial. As I gaze at the carved objects I have made, Michael's experience in New Guinea floods my consciousness. I know in this moment I will have to do more; I will have to reenact his death in ceremony if I am to touch and release that place in me that will not let him go. I must do this before I commemorate his life.

Near my foot lies a beautiful, curled piece of aspen bark. I open it up and cut into it with my knife, shaping it into an Asmat long boat canoe. The marsh behind the glen that I had discovered the day I found my power spot will represent the swampy lowlands of the New Guinea coast and the river delta where Michael's boat capsized and was carried by the current out to sea.

MARSH DEATH CEREMONY

The ceremony opens spontaneously at the marsh. In a small, broken voice I sing "Eternal Father, Strong to Save," and weep at the last line: "For those in peril on the sea." Through my tears I search for a symbol of Michael. All around me, gray moss hangs from the dying pines, whose roots are planted in the wet soil at the edge of the water. I pick a small bunch of the moss and place it in the bottom of the canoe, and then cover it with a piece of maidenhair fern that encloses a wild columbine flower, its purple and white petals, a crown.

Gently, the canoe enters the dark water; I push it off from the shore. There is no breeze and little current. The boat loses momentum and stops, resting against some reeds about three feet from the shore. I close my eyes and whisper, "Michael." I am not sure I hear my voice. My eyes open, seeking the boat—hoping it is gone—finding it there, caught like my gaze in the same reeds. Time seems to stop—sight blurs—then from above, a whirring sound breaks through my fog, ending the spell. Swift flight and flashing color announce a hummingbird. The numbness that has been spreading within me breaks. Where I was caught staring hopelessly at the stuck funereal canoe, I am now freed, able to rise and walk along the edge of the marsh. I stop where it meets the tiny pond and step up on a solid, grassy mound. It's dry here, but still next to the water, next to Michael's truth. Here I can stand; here I will give my testimony.

MEMORIAL TESTAMENT—THE MARSH POND

I am here, Mike, standing at the water, marking your truth—your death—so I might let you go. I still don't want to, despite everything . . . You are part of and yet so separate from me. I can't find you—how can I let you go?

I start again.

I am here, standing up for you, Mike, for us—bearing witness to our life together, to your life in me, with me, and on your own.

I've had dreams—with Jeremy—they must be about you, about us. We are in an early place of floating, of holding . . .

I have no sense of "I," only "we," in these dreams. I think it's why I don't remember "you" or "me" when we were very little.

Sometimes I've thought the pain must come to me from another planet, that I was crazy, and it was all an illusion, us being so close— our early day and night lives constantly intertwined, crazy because we grew up and into such separate worlds.

It helps now to have Mom's and Pat's descriptions of us as babies and toddlers. Recently, I saw the two of us in a home movie. We were about two years old. You were so cute, Mike, with your round, curious face and straight hair, me with my curls—both of us, delighted. We wore matching sun suits, holding two small parasols as we ran around in and out of each other's reach; going out and coming back, as if we held each other on a yoyo at the end of a string.

I can feel you, Geedie, when I don't remember you—I can't describe it—it's like the feelings are coming from my cells. I can hardly find the good feelings. Mostly it's a missing—a terrible ache. I think there must be a body memory quite separate from the mind.

I wonder what we called each other when we first started to talk. Maybe Grannie Clark inadvertently gave us our names. Do you remember when she held us on her lap and played Geetsie, Guytsie, the two spiders who crawl up your arms? She would tickle us into fits of giggles. Somehow Guytsie got lost and Geetsie became Geedie, and that is what we've called each other ever since.

This name—Geedie—felt like an "anchor to windward" to me when we were growing up. It was a lifeline, holding us together, present for us alone, even when we were physically separated.

Roddy picked it up, calling us both "Geedies." He still does it. "Hi, Geedies," he says, and kisses me. It brings a bit of you back. No one else remembers. I know it is a silly-sounding name. But I am so touched by it.

I want to bring back our early life together now.

Remember our little twin bedroom at the end of the old part of the house in Washington? I can see it: There were two steps up out of our room to the landing, which opened into the bathroom and Pat's room. Beyond her room were the back stairs and the screened-in sleeping porch where we took our naps. Those naps, Mike . . . we loved the bumblebees . . .

When I talked to Pat last spring, she told me you were always the adventurous one—walking months before me. I was content to just sit and play, she said. You were a dreadful tease, Mike, even then.

What about the brown flower you told me was growing on the wallpaper above your bed, the one you reached up to touch and then dared me to climb up and touch, too? When I finally did, the flower moved! Pat came in and screamed. It was a huge spider. I think she was scared to death and took it out on me. You got away with it, as usual. Pat put the straps on me, attaching them to the bed so I wouldn't be able to come over and get into yours. I've been scared of spiders ever since.

I can just see us when we learned to brush our teeth, standing on our little stools by the sink. The trick was to get Dr. Lyon's Tooth Powder wet before it fell off the toothbrush. You mostly swallowed the paste. "No, Michael, spit, spit!" Pat would say. Remember the little bun at the back of her head and the way her nose dripped when it got cold?

I can't think of anything we did alone before we were separated when we were five or six. Then Mom put me in a room on the other side of Pat. I could not get to you at night when I was scared. I was not even allowed a light.

It was the beginning of a very bad time for me, Geedie. And you? What was it like for you? We never talked about it growing up. I wonder if you were as scared and lonely as I was when they took me away from you. I somehow think it wasn't as bad for you, at least, not after we moved back to New York. Looking over your short life, it's as if you had so much to accomplish. You couldn't look back—you had to move forward.

When we moved to the city apartment, I was horrified to find your bedroom was next to Steven's and on a different floor from mine. Then you both were sent to Buckley School. He was to be your new playmate— what a shock. My going to Brearley School with Ann did not help, either. The four years' age difference seemed like a lifetime. Sometimes Ann was mean. And she was downstairs next to Steven. I was left out.

We were never allowed to be together in the same way again—just us, complete in our own world. From our parents, from Pat, from school, the message was clear—you were a boy and I was a girl. Forget being twins. We were to bond with our own sex. The "cute twin thing" no longer applied.

Honestly, I was angry at you for not standing up for me, Mike. Why didn't you protest—throw a real tantrum, do something? My squawks and tears impressed no one—yours might have mattered.

What a big deal when Pat left when we were ten. I loved being allowed to walk home alone from the school bus—three blocks for me, twelve for you. My big adventure entailed wandering along Madison Avenue, looking in the news store for forbidden comic books and stopping at the drugstore for an ice-cream soda when I'd saved enough allowance.

But you were already reaching for a wider world. One time you came home so late that Mother almost called the police. When you finally arrived, oblivious of the time, you happily told us about your visit to "Harry," who was teaching you about paintings. Do you remember? Mom met you at school the next day and you went together to see Harry Yot-nakparian at his Old Master's Gallery on Madison Avenue. Apparently you were drawn to a painting in his second-floor window, went to the side door, and rang the gallery's bell until Harry let you up. Mom said Harry talked about you as a serious boy eager to learn about art. I was amazed that they let you go back whenever you wanted—as long as you were not in Harry's way and got yourself home on time. I think Mother and Father were proud of you. It is a family story now, Geedie. We love to tell it about you.

I have a portfolio of your paintings from grade school and college. They are really good. You drew a beautiful reclining nude, which I framed. The big deal was the painting of Jesus that you made in Sunday school. It still hangs in the hall outside the rectory. When tourists go to see the

Chagall and Matisse windows in the church, the minister shows them your painting and tells about how Chagall was impressed by your work. When I take friends to that church, I still feel proud of you.

Well, I wanted to be a singer. You probably don't remember, but I sang a solo in The Mikado and got into the special choral group at Madeira. My secret fantasy was to sing the blues in a smoky dive. I would sit on the washing machine in the basement of the dorm at Madeira pretending it was a piano, and I was crooning into a mike in a long, slinky gown.

Would you have continued to paint? Would you have been a collector like Father, and an architect? I could not believe he didn't let you major in architecture at Harvard.

"College is a time to build your foundation," he said. "Study history or economics." Why weren't you more upset, Mike? Why did you acquiesce to what he said?

God, I'm still getting out from under Father! Is that part of what you were doing by going to New Guinea? An unspoken agenda—but with his blessing? Yet what would he have expected from you when you got back? Would you then have gone your own way?

I mustn't go there, Geedie. What if? What if? There aren't any ifs; isn't that the point!?

But you know, in rare moments, when I manage to get underneath the grief, I sense, even dare to feel, that your life was complete.

An aching back induces me to sit down on a nearby rock to rest and drink from my water bottle. I watch the pond spread out in uneven patches of sun and shade. I wonder about Michael's canoe. My eyes close over tears. Slowly, the whine of gathering mosquitoes interrupts. Then, another sound, a hum, a delicate throb. My eyes blink open to brown and iridescent green. The hummingbird hovers two inches from my face. For a second, it seems to stand in the air. I hear a single, high chirp—he's gone. He evaporates my tears and lifts my spirit. I feel able to remember Mike again.

There is more about grade school, Geedie—about you and me becoming separate. As you began to shift your focus outward, I still held on to you. I did not let go. I worried a lot when you had what Mother called "growing pains" and then the "juvenile migraines." When the headaches came, it seemed like you spent endless hours in a dark room, waiting for the pain to pass. Once, I had to hold on to you on the train platform. Do you remember? We were on the way to visit Granny and Granpop Clark in Philadelphia. I wouldn't let Pat touch you; I led you to your seat because the migraine made you temporarily blind. You were such a good sport, Geedie. You never complained.

By the time we were ten, I had grown several inches taller than you. I was upset. You must have been a bit upset, too, because Mom told me when we were introduced to guests you would say, "This is my twin sister, Mary, and she is taller than I am."

When we had family pictures taken that summer in Maine, I bent my knees so we would be remembered as being the same height. The photographer pointed it out to Mother, who told me to straighten up. I know you heard her, Mike. I was mortified to think everyone would focus on you being shorter than me—too small for your age. All that worry, Geedie, and you ended up 5'10"—two inches taller than me. . . .

You know, I can't sense much worry in your personality. That is one of the special things about you, the specialness of you that began appearing back then. I think it will take a lot of my life to drop the worrying; I must have carried it for you, too.

Mainly, I remember your good spirits and your impish sense of humor, especially when it came to teasing me. That wasn't always so great. In those days I was really jealous of Steven—he took you away from me. He was jealous of me, too; he told me so last year, especially when you wouldn't go along with his teasing. When he got too mean, you just sidestepped his plans, moving to my side in an undramatic way. Except for you, we all fought a lot as kids. Somehow, in that competitive tug of war, you remained untouched.

How different we were becoming. I have always tended to get emotionally involved—fighting back if I felt I, or someone else, was wronged.

"All right, Miss Righteous Indignation," Father used to say. Remember?

Your caring showed in such a different manner from mine. I was interacting and reacting, trying to change things. You were observing, skirting conflict, choosing the nourishing experience—embracing life, absorbing, reaching out to include others in whatever you delighted in.

Within the pain of our separation I misunderstood your independence and our growing differences. When the rest of our family was grappling with emotional and behavioral issues and the tension built, your absence troubled me. I felt abandoned; felt you did not love me as much as I loved you. I wanted you there, pitching in at my side. I longed for our old bond. And "telling it like it was" got me in a lot of trouble. Perhaps you escaped some of the emotional wounding by leaving the scene or staying quiet. It was smart not to stick out. In stepping back, you saw more than one side of the argument, and you didn't take everything so seriously as I did.

I will never forget you, Geedie, before Rod's wedding. Mom was in an emotional crise about us getting ready on time and being properly dressed. We were finally piling into the cars when we noticed you were not there.

After much searching and calling, someone found you up behind the guesthouse, on the lawn, dressed in your tuxedo, practicing your golf swing. Mom's subsequent outcry sailed right over your head. With that impish look on your face, you pinched me when you got into the car. The memory of it still makes me want to giggle.

You know, you often seemed focused elsewhere—connecting with everything around you. It was visual. Even when we walked together, you had trouble staying beside me. What a pain, Geedie. When we were going somewhere together in New York, I'd suddenly notice you were gone, and then turned to find you behind me down the block looking at some old object in a crowded store window. Or, if we were in the country, you might peel off to the side of the road, and I would find you peering at two intersecting branches that made an intriguing shape against the sky.

When I was home, I was painfully aware of our separation. But I experienced a huge change in the image I had of myself as separate from you when I went away to the Madeira School. There, I felt appreciated and supported. At Madeira, I really began to venture out and flourish on my own. And you, at Exeter—I know you did well there, but I wish I remembered how it was for you when you first left home.

It was big stuff, when we each began to date. What fun we had! Your friends became my friends and my boyfriends, too. You even dated my roommate, Meme, at Vassar, remember? You often came home on vacation with Wat and Sam or John. And I loved going to Exeter for special weekends. I found plenty of my own mischievous energy then, to match yours. The best times were in college. Do you remember the ski weekend in Vail when we climbed on the roof of the neighboring ski lodge and put a blanket over the chimney, sending the after-ski party reeling out into the snow?

But you were oblivious, too, Geedie, and sometimes wildly irritating—like when you stopped to pick up a soldier in your little two-seater Studebaker on the way to Stowe, Vermont. I was next to you and our skis were jammed in diagonally from the back of the car to the front, right to the windshield. I could not believe my eyes when you suddenly pulled off the road and offered this soldier a ride. The only place for him to sit was in my seat with me on his lap. I was so pissed at you, Geedie. How dumb was I? I should have refused to go along with it. I can just hear you laughing—it's still not funny.

God, there are so many memories. I guess the most important thing was our talks together, the way we would listen and just know each other, understanding and accepting each other's thoughts and opinions without a need for explanation. I don't have that with anyone else. I loved the long hours we spent discussing the meaning of our lives and how we must find out who we were outside of our family. You were wonderful, telling me we had to get jobs working with people who did not recognize our name or give a damn if they did.

We got those jobs, too—you went to the Llanos in Venezuela, to work on a cattle ranch; I went to the Navajo reservation, to join a health research project run by Cornell. Every time a reporter mentioned me in the newspaper in my early adult years, he would write that I "worked with Indians, lived in a trailer, and ate out of cans." Well, I guess I did, but it's more important to me now that I worked as part of a rural health service and research team. We both loved the challenge of that summer. I'll bet your job whetted your appetite for an experience like New Guinea.

I want to remember with you our trip together after Steven's wedding in Norway, the summer before our senior year. We bought funny lithographs—mine, a group of tipsy Vikings on old knobbly horses, and yours, a group of crazy, wild-eyed imaginary animals flying in through one door and out another. In Copenhagen, you encouraged me to purchase my first real piece of art—a beautiful oil painting of the highlands of Denmark. That painting hangs in my house in South Salem. I love it as much as when we saw it in the store window and I dared buy it.

It was great, Mike, wandering to our heart's content, just us, not needing anyone else. How neat being able to sit up half the night in a smoky café, sharing our lives, talking about Mother and Father, and and their influences on our characters. You thought Mom set the standards:

truthfulness, loyalty, integrity, the fact there are no shortcuts to doing the right thing, plus all those overwhelming "shoulds" and "oughts" of our culture, most of which you said you floated with and I have often felt swamped by. But Mom also gave us our sense of humor and mischievousness. She keeps it hidden a lot, but when it shows—like when she ran naked with Ann and me out over the lawn after skinny-dipping in the pool in the dark—I was so thrilled. I'll never forget.

We decided Father shaped our view of the world as exciting and worth finding out about. He and Grandfather also set the expectations, narrowed down to one essential word—stewardship, giving back to society what we have been given. It's so heavy. Father did everything in huge, broad strokes—his plans, his work, his success. We felt such pressure to do that, too. I haven't been able to deal very well with that pressure. One thing I'm glad of is you don't have to have it anymore. Being a Rockefeller, I mean—giving back in that huge arena. I am happiest when I work with a tiny piece of the world, preferably with small groups or one-on-one. I am going back to school, Geedie, to Columbia to get my master's to become a psychotherapist. Just like you said, I am going to work where no one will need to know about our family, where it is not an issue, and where I can really help.

Father would never admit to being affected by a setback or a failure. Right after he had lost the nomination for President in 1964, with that terrible scene at the Republican National Convention, I told him I was so sorry about what happened to him. He simply replied, "It's not a problem, Mary; it's just another challenge." I do not believe that. And after he lost to Nixon in 1968, it was the end of his dream. Those losses, and finding himself a neutered vice president under Ford, left him dispirited. He never recovered. I wish you'd been there and we could have talked about it. Maybe he would have talked to you. Father's attitude has made it more difficult for me to face my feelings and my failures.

But I remember we both appreciated the wonderful influence of Father's enthusiasm, his creativity, and his love of art. I think that love gave him the joy he took from life. You inherited all that from him. And your willingness to work hard, Geedie, and do the job well—you got that from Father and Mother. Father loved in you all those good qualities, and all that you gave back.

In many ways, you are a blithe spirit, serious about your life yet so happy with its adventure. I know you and Sam first wanted to go to New Guinea because you both craved the adventure of exploring the unknown—mastering a wild, remote terrain, and getting to know a way of life and a people totally foreign to your sensibilities. I have to admit, it was perfect for you, perfect for finding out about yourself without the family and for exploring your love of art.

You can't imagine how important the New Guinea collection has become, as well as the whole new wing at the Met. How it has enhanced the knowledge and appreciation of Asmat and Oceanic art . . . really, all indigenous art. And the fellowship at Harvard—your life now stands as an example to the recipients of the importance of breaking out of an American view of the world, of finding a new perspective. Your life has given these kids a real chance to find their own paths.

When I have been frightened at the daunting task of this vision quest, I think of you on the anthropological expedition to the Balim Valley. You stayed a difficult course, learned your trade, and did a great job of sound recording for the film, even when you had dreamed of being the photographer and Sam got the job instead. I am so proud of the way you handled the anger, guilt, and despair you shared with me at having to stay professionally removed when your team's intervention might have prevented a death in the tribe you were observing. And, of course, you were brave, holding your microphone in a ditch between two warring tribes to get the best sound recording—I have the arrow you got in your *leg. But it's not your bravery, Mike—it's the way you persevered and became a valued team member, rising to do your part in a challenging and new situation, and how you grew from all of it—that's what has given me courage on this trip.*

A frog leaps into the pond, making me jump. I watch his liquid trail. It's hot. I place my hand in the water, letting it float through the coolness.

When I see my hand, I miss yours, Geedie. It's the only part of you I still have a clear picture of—your wide palms and short fingers and the particular rounded shape of your nails. You know, I have one fingernail that looks like yours.

I miss the way you hold and look at things, as if your curiosity leaves your eyes and becomes your hands.

Oh God, Mike, I miss not being able to share ever again, or laugh together and joke with our friends. It's so hard to accept that there is and will be no future for our own families together, no playing of our kids. It's never going to happen. I know it—I want you to hear me say it. . . .

There is still more—the hardest part. Turning inward to my imagery world, I ask my mountain lion and my dog Oliver to come and lie beside me. I can feel their warm, solid flanks against my legs.

I have got to talk about my feelings about Father and Mother's divorce and about New Guinea—to make things right between us, Mike, I have to share the whole truth.

You know I was dead set against your decision to go to such a dangerous and remote place. Father championed the whole idea, so there was no way I could change your mind. I had a premonition then that you would die.

When Father told Mother he wanted a divorce, you had finished one

Asmat trip, and you came all the way home to see them. You called me in San Diego, remember? We argued about our parents—actually, I got upset and angry. I did not want to hear your opinion, your perspective; your interest in seeing the situation from both their points of view. I felt Father was wrong. He left Mother for another woman, and asked Mom, after thirty years of loyalty, to bear the burden and go to Reno. Those were the facts as I saw them—period.

To think I could have taken a plane home to see you, Mike—I didn't think of it as a possibility. I am so sorry for that now and for my reaction to our phone conversation. I could have disagreed with you without a fight. I could have at least taken in the gift of your voice after so long. I didn't . . .

Then, when I heard you were lost, some place I've kept hidden in me was furious with Father and you, too. This helpless anger came from the fact that on some deepest level, I knew my premonition had come true.

And there's something else—

I can't believe, Mike, that you didn't leave the catamaran when it swamped, especially when the two young guides—local people who knew the river and its currents—told you they must swim ashore. I know you wanted to save your camera equipment and film, your valuable field notes, maybe some small sculptures. But was all that worth your life?

Now, all these years later, I am letting my anger go. I think your optimism and your drive to carry out your mission caused you to miss the dire reality.. But oh God, Mike—you were carried out to sea, miles from shore with no means of communication, no food or water, no hope of rescue . . .

You chose to swim. This decision feels different—different from any other decision you ever made. René told Father and me he couldn't really swim. You risked your life to save him, to save you both. I am deeply proud and respectful. And I am awed that this immense decision was not made in a kind of heroic reaction. You had twelve hours to think of your options, to ponder the consequences, and to make your choice. I see now that you made your final choice, steeped in the Asmat environment where you'd found life and death exposed and intertwined with everyday reality. It's so hard to take that in. I am used to all the hiding, denying, and glorifying that covers death up as soon as it surfaces.

I want to walk with you, Michael, to bear witness to what happened, to know your fear, your courage, your pain. I cannot. I have to free us both, complete myself and you without ever knowing what really happened. Now, when I dare to uncover your death—when I dare to watch you start to swim—I see you disappear into the horizon. You are gone, Michael. The final truth is—your beautiful life is gone.

When I rise from the rock to leave the marsh, I know I will not return. Sadness seeps from me, filling the glen and merging with the very air I breathe.

CHAPTER TWENTY-FOUR

I SAT BEFORE the mossy burial stump. The truth had to be honored in a loving act of respect—I needed to commit Michael's body that lay within my heart, to this earth. The burial site welcomed me, holding up its forms of life and death woven within the delicate carpet of the forest floor. There in the soft soil at the heart of the stump, I buried five symbols of Michael, his life, and the love that encircled him: a beautiful flat stone I found on the Medicine Walk, a cowry shell from the Asmat, a sea shell with a hole in it from Maine, Ann's citrine stone, and one of Michael's letters.

BURIAL CEREMONY

The earth below feels rich and light in my hands. It receives and embraces the objects. My hands know the earth before I do—as if they know the touch of our mother. I thank the Great God Mystery and ask it to receive

Mike's spirit from his body that I am releasing—to receive it through the hole in the seashell and then from the back of the crow. The space around the grave feels full of presence. I recognize those who might be gathered here—Mike's friends and family and loved ones, especially Sally, Michael's girlfriend. Behind my closed eyes, the snake from the base of my spine dances an undulating dance. It weaves itself through the soil and among the objects until the grave takes the shape of a nest. The snake then glides slowly from the grave, swaying gracefully, bending with respect to all who gather there before vanishing beneath the pine needles and leafy undergrowth. I offer an ending prayer for my twin, and gently fill in the grave with the earth I had removed that morning, placing pine needles on top and some old pine cones and a piece of bark that looks a bit like Mike's longboat canoe. Everything is left as if it had always been there, except for a tiny bunch of flowers, the small Asmat shields, and the bis pole, all arranged together as a headstone. There is a sacred stillness in the air around the burial site.

THIRD DAY—BEFORE DAWN

Stream sounds and the first birds—intermittent, timorous twittering. The glen washed in palest gray. Above my head, four clear notes: one low, three high; the first one slow, and the next three fast—the purest, sweetest sound.

"Hello, Mary."
"Hello, blessed morning."
Eyes brimming, soft tears—no pain.
My animals appear, crowding into my mind before my thoughts and worries can enter. This is the final day of letting Michael go—where the place in me that grasps onto him, to his life, must die as he did.

Coyote comes to me first. He doesn't smile. He licks my streaming face. He bays to the descending moon, calling all the animals and spirits to come close and bear witness. With a strange flapping, the bat flies in and lights on my shoulder. Silently he rises, circling my power spot, clearing all energetic impediments. Returning, he settles again on my shoulder. I touch his delicate wings with tenderness. There is no blood on his mouth. The little white butterfly, the being from my throat, lands on my hand. She tells me to bring two flowers to the ceremony, to remind me that in dying I will be reborn.

Rabbit waits quietly. He's lying down. The dove glides in to land beside him. She and the rabbit repeat their message: Peace. Peace is the key to becoming reborn as the two separate flowers that grew on the bush by the stream on the Medicine Walk—one for Michael, one for me. The animals look gravely at me. I sense the promise held within the word peace.

"You have made a good start in dealing with your feelings about death," says Rabbit. "You will finish that today when you realize the value of what you no longer need."

I try to understand. My cat Sunny's words come back. "Just let feelings come and be who you are. That's enough."

THIRD DAY—10 A.M.: A DEATH LODGE

I am drawn to a spot surrounded by fallen trees. Dead limbs protrude from one tree, which I cover with my poncho, making a shelter. Directly in front of the entrance grows a wild geranium plant with two flowers on it—two living flowers, like those on the rose bush. My body just fits between and under the sharp protrusions of the dead pine limbs. I sit with my knees to my chest, my head down. With my arms crossed, I hide my face and hands from the gathering mosquitoes.

Outwardly I'm silent. Inwardly, I speak to the left side of my body that waits to heal from the pain, the loss of feeling, and the injury it has been prone to since Michael died. I speak of the emptiness, of feeling incomplete without my twin, of loneliness, longing, and sadness. I acknowledge that it is this shriveled side of myself that must die, this fake skin under which I still hide. Although I have buried Michael in the earth, somehow I have not yet released him fully from inside.

Be who you are, Mary, Sunny whispers. *It is enough.*

A sudden, warm breeze carries the smell of pine.

Dear God, Dear Great Oneness, that holds me and all that is: Michael's death has forced upon me the opportunity to truly discover myself, and the opportunity to feel at home, alone and safe, as a separate and distinct person. Let me release the part of Mike that no longer exists so I might truly live that opportunity.

For a long time it is quiet—inside and out—then the hum, throb, and high chirp of the hummingbird.

THIRD DAY—RESTING IN MY TENT

Rain begins to tap at my tent flap. In the background, thunder rises above the sound of the stream. With a chirp, a tiny bird streaks across my view. That's four times since I've been here. I decide to talk to this hummingbird—

The imagery world opens quickly. The little bird keeps time with his wings in front of my face. He says he is the spirit of my power spot, and that forever, when I see a hummingbird, I must remember my power spot and what has taken place here.

THIRD DAY—4:30 P.M.

I've got to go to the rock pile and then maybe eat something and begin to collect my things for tomorrow when I return to base camp. I'll need to change into warm clothes, for I have decided to do a burning and letting-go ritual at sundown, and then enter my circle of stones to begin my rebirth—or at least ask it to begin. I remember my babies' births. They certainly did not start until they were good and ready!

When the Native American peoples cried for a vision of rebirth, they would stay outside and awake all night in their sacred spots. I'm not going to ask this of myself. I'm not up for staying outside all night completely unprotected in the dark. I'll get up just before dawn and pray that will suffice.

BURNING CEREMONY

I can't get the fire started, no matter how small the sticks. I've even cheated by using paper. Afraid I'll run out of matches, I use the Sterno.

This burning ceremony is difficult for me because of its significance. I have done so much to prepare for it—I'm emotionally drained. It feels anticlimactic. Part of me seems present, part watches.

As the sun begins to set, I burn the final letter I received from Michael, my last connection to his voice, to his hand. I tear up the letter piece by piece before releasing it into the fire.

"I love you, Mike. I'm letting you go so you can be free, so you can be whole."

I repeat this over and over as I drop each piece into the flames. When the last piece burns, I get out the symbol for Mike and me together. It's a maple seed pod, shaped like two wings stuck together, the type I used to break open as a kid, sticking one wing on either side of my nose. I drop it, still joined, into the fire.

"We are now separate but whole, separate and still loving each other."

Gently I take the beech leaf from the box. I stare at its yellow right side and then at the left shriveled side that has turned from brown to gray; it disintegrates as I let it fall into the fire.

"I allow this side of me to die now, the side that would not thrive or grow without you, Michael."

I stand. My intention is strong.

May we both be reborn.

I write these words down in what is left of the firelight from the Sterno. A flying bug swoops by my face. Taking a closer look at it, I see it is a tiny white moth—my white butterfly—here in the dark reminding me that death and rebirth are intertwined.

THIRD DAY—EVENING

It is after eight o'clock when I step into my circle of stones dressed in all my warm clothes. The rapidly receding daylight behind the trees creates long shadows that crisscross the glen. I watch them fade into the coming darkness. A sudden crash deep in the woods is followed by a series of receding sounds of breaking branches. It's probably just a deer; but then the noise is awfully loud . . . Gone is my sense of the ubiquitous harmony between me and all who share these woods. I've been so lucky; no bears or mountain lions, not even a porcupine or skunk, have wanted to share my tent. I realize, with a shaky breath, that to an angry or even curious bear, my tent, with its zippered screen or snapped waterproof flaps, would be like a cracker box—it would never prevent an attack. I feel unprotected from the night or the animals.

Panicked, with nowhere to run, I huddle in the middle of the circle and try to breathe, to feel the support of the earth and listen to the stream. I don't know whether to keep my eyes open or shut. The night has rushed into the glen, leaving nothing but darkening shadows that take on new and ominous shapes.

I hear Steve's voice: "Ask the night what it needs from you."

I get an immediate reaction—the distinct feeling that the night has come as a blanket for the Earth and all who inhabit it, that it is a protective cover to enable most of life to rest.

The night tells me I need to breathe it into myself and allow it to cover me so it might replace the phony darkness I have been imagining.

I breathe and breathe, slowing my breath—the fear recedes. No strange mountain lion, bear, or bobcat appears, only my imagery animals, Mountain Lion and now Oliver, who both come into my journey and lie down along the sides of the circle, filling me with their strength. When I am quiet inside, Oliver stands and gravely announces he has come now as Michael's animal of imagery, a partner to the mountain lion who is mine. He will stay with Michael until the end of my quest. They tell me to begin the ceremony of rebirth and to continue to breathe in the sweet darkness of the glen.

I slide down flat on the earth and then curl up, imagining my body in the snake's nest. I meditate on the snake's eggs, on keeping them warm, especially the one with me inside.

Nothing more happens. It is very dark and begins to rain. When I get up from the circle, I need my flashlight to find my way back to the tent. I am not scared, but cannot sleep. Doubts come. This quest may all be a trick of my will and imagination. I block these thoughts and try to concentrate over and over on breathing in the protective darkness, asking it to allow me to sleep.

FOURTH DAY—2 A.M.

Dream 1: A man comes near to me in a murderous stance and with wild eyes. I hear Sam's and Steve's words: "Ask him what he wants from you."

The man says he wants to kill me. I tell him he can't. Is there anything else he wants? He says, "Some clothes." I give him mine.

Dream 2: I am in and out of ticket offices. I've lost my tickets and my purse. I am with my cousin Jay (he was wonderful to me after Michael was lost). I am supposed to go somewhere with Jay, but everything is mixed up . . . I can't remember.

FOURTH DAY—PREDAWN IN MY TENT

It's black outside. My flashlight illuminates my watch: 4:15. I close my eyes and offer affirmations and prayers, asking for courage and the gift of rebirth. It's still drizzling. I roll on my back and bring my knees to my chest, struggling to get on my rain pants and, finally, my jacket and boots, while trying not to kick over the little tent and the flashlight. I unsnap the tent flaps. Morning light is barely visible.

In the circle of stones I curl back into the fetal position, imagining that I am warming the eggs. I concentrate on the left side of my body, visualizing it making a new arm and leg, a new buttock, and a new half of my face. I'm very afraid nothing will happen. I cannot seem to ask what needs to happen and then focus inside and wait. It is so hard now to trust this process, to allow rather than to create. Dispirited, I turn to the sky to wait for the dawn, for a new day.

My eyes close; I am so tired I almost think I am asleep and it is a dream. I feel the presence of my snake. I ask her how I can get out of my shell.

"Simple," she says, "if it won't crack open by pushing, kick out with your two feet at once. Do the same with your hands."

The egg's shell feels tight around my body. It's difficult to breathe. I push and push—nothing happens. I thrust out, my legs and arms exploding in unison. The egg cracks open. I sit up.

There are no big feelings—just an inner smile, which emerges with the breaking day.

I pray that my crow has taken what I held of Michael and his spirit back to him, and that Michael is now whole.

CHAPTER TWENTY-FIVE

I AM BACK at the base camp on the little hill, tired and thrilled I could make it up the rise with my pack after four days of almost no food. The guides, Ann, and other questers cheered as I wobbled and puffed. No one helped me. It is my victory!

I carefully left the glen as I had found it, except for the markers on Michael's grave. My immense gratitude for my beautiful, powerful spot and the experience I had there is touched with sadness. Part of me feels bereft at having left the new home I found in nature, which I never dreamed could exist for me. I struggle with my need to hold on to this precious place, trying to take the gift into the fabric of myself, and then letting what has finished go.

AFTER WE GOT settled around the fire, we recounted our solo journeys, listening to each other, hearing ourselves. I was immensely proud that I had completed my quest and that I was able to take care of myself during those few days in the wilderness. I realized with new confidence that I never felt the need to talk to or call Steve. As a matter of fact, I have had a difficult transition from the quiet of my campsite with its natural sounds to the constant, happy chattering of my spirited fellow questers. Yet, I'm relieved to be back—it is so good to eat!

BACK AT THE LODGE—LAST NIGHT OF QUEST

With nourishment and sleep and the help of our four human guides to bring closure to our solo experiences, the hike back to the waiting jeeps held no untoward challenges, and the reentry into a larger world began to feel more natural.

Before we broke camp, at the last talking staff sharing around the campfire, I voiced concern as to whether I truly had accomplished my goal of letting Michael go. I could not feel a clear answer inside. Instead, I found a kind of blank space—just not filled in. One of the vision quest guides told me it was not unusual to feel unfinished after one's quest. It often took months, even years, for the changes to be completely understood. My new life could not mature all at once. It would slowly grow, and would need to be tried and tested many times before being fully integrated.

Back at the lodge, I gratefully took a long shower, washed my clothes, and repacked my backpack for the journey home. Gathering again as a group, we continued the process of taking in what we had accomplished and taking stock of what we had learned. We discussed ways to successfully reenter our communities and steps to bring about our new purpose for life.

On that final day, with the morning sun pouring across the wood floor of the meeting hall, we formed a circle with Steve for one last imagery journey.

This journey would mark the end of the vision quest. My eyes filled as they closed. I wondered with some trepidation whether my imagery would tell me if I had finished my quest. Steve's sonorous voice called in the stillness and led the way.

Mountain Lion comes and takes me on her back. We walk to the marsh at the back of the glen. As we enter the water it becomes the ocean. The lion's body lengthens as she swims. I merge with Michael, who is there in the water on Oliver's back. We leave Oliver and Mountain Lion and swim off as one. We swim and swim. We swim until we tire and sink beneath the waves. I feel no panic, no fear, no pain. I know I must take the water into my lungs. My body turns over and over until I can relax, breathe in the water, and then start to float, deep in the sea. Moving with the current, I begin to disintegrate.

Lost, I call to my mountain lion for help. She reappears. She takes me up and lays me down on the beach. I am no longer a part of my twin. Next to my body is Michael's skull.

I rest, safe in the curve of Elephant's trunk. Later, I lie between Mountain Lion's paws and watch as my butterfly circles round and round the skull. Rabbit hops in a circle around it, too. Deer comes forward and touches the skull with her nose. She is fully grown. The Crow appears. He swoops down and lands on the dome of the skull and pecks the eye sockets clean, making them ready for a different kind of seeing. Bat is there, too, flying back and forth, cleaning the air above.

This preparation ends when my elephant gently scoops up the skull and cradles it with her trunk. The animals gather round as she places the skull on the ground in front of Oliver, who has grown as large as Mountain Lion. Oliver pushes the skull into a hole he had dug and paws dirt over it until it is entirely covered. Elephant then bears her full weight onto her front right foot, placed upon this new mound of earth. It flattens to the level of the ground. Elephant steps back; we wait.

Soon a sphere of white light rises up from the grave. It floats slowly to the back of the crow. Crow's wings spread and he lifts upward until he is over the sea, rising higher and higher with the sphere of light. When he is high enough, the bright orb leaves his back and travels on alone. We watch it until it disappears, merging with the light of the sky.

We gaze upward for a long time. My heart is huge. I hear my words: "Dearest Mike, goodbye."

PART FOUR

Moving Forward

CHAPTER TWENTY-SIX

The crow picks the skull's eyes clean, making it ready for a new kind of seeing: Michael's death, my death, new eyes, a new vision.

UPON REENTERING THE outside world that summer of 1988, I focused on the last goal of the vision quest: to bring the gift of new vision back to my community. *Who are the people I will do this for?* I wondered. *Who is my community?* I was not sure, yet I knew this community had to be big enough to hold all those who were trapped in denial, fear, and isolation like I had been, and those who were caught in pain and in separation from their deeper, feeling selves.

On my solo, I had shared with Michael my decision to become a psychotherapist. Before the vision quest, however, I knew that this would not be possible until I healed the wound of my loss and let Michael go. Now I had something to give. I became a clinical social worker in 1991.

For a year, I worked in a state-supported social service agency, doing therapy with individuals, parents and children. Although I loved the people I worked with, I felt there was too much paperwork, too much focus on making and documenting treatment plans, and not enough time spent in being fully present for the needs of clients. I decided to go it on my own. With the psychiatrist I went to after Father's death as a supervisor, I opened a private practice in late 1992. Steve Gallegos had started training imagery guides. In the fall, after I received my master's in social work, I signed up for one of his courses and studied with him for six years, until I became a certified guide and trainer.

About two years into my private practice, I met a twinless twin. Brian came to me for therapy at the request of his distraught father. He had been present when his twin brother was murdered during his senior year in college. Brian waited six months after his father called me before making an appointment. In my office, he paced back and forth, telling me that everything he knew about psychotherapy had come from watching television. He did not like what he had seen.

"Anyway," he added, "how would you know what I feel—you have no idea what it is like to be or lose a twin."

Admiration for this young man's ability to share his strong true feelings was my first reaction—so different from my own inability to speak the truth with Dr. Simmons. Then I remembered my training; it discouraged a therapist from sharing personal experience with clients. I took a deep breath.

"I can't know what your unique experience has been," I answered. "But I can share with you that I am a twin, and that my twin died. Also, that I had a lonely, painful, and protracted healing journey, partly because I met no one who understood me, and no one who shared the experience of losing a twin."

Brian looked at me for the first time. He came over to the chair next to mine and sat down. In the following weeks, we walked together on his special healing path. I was deeply touched by the way he slowly moved to confront, integrate, and reframe the helpless horror of his twin's and his own experience, and by his finally being able to take in the experience as finished. We worked with imagery, his inner guides always leading and keeping him safe as he confronted and dealt with his tumultuous feelings. With therapeutic support, Brian was able to navigate around the seductive trap of bitterness. He came to a place where he was able to look forward to becoming a doctor and to the possibilities of an individual life, able to carry within him the enduring love from and for his twin.

By my second session with Brian, I knew that carrying out my vision meant working with twins—bereaved twins. But there seemed no way to reach these twins. Professionally, it felt wrong to advertise. It was before the time of websites and social networking. I shared my feelings with colleagues, hoping for a referral, but no one knew a twinless twin. My practice kept me busy and engaged while my fervent hope and vision slowly faded.

On the morning of September 11, 2001, the world of all Americans changed. The day after the World Trade Center towers collapsed, I made my way down to Bellevue Hospital to volunteer. The hospital was overloaded with the wounded; anxious relatives and friends of the missing waited outside in long lines, all hoping to find news of their loved ones. The administrative staff put my name in their database, but I never heard from them. I had also signed up with the Red Cross, which was eager to recruit professional psychological support. However, it was only interested in therapists working eight-hour shifts, and I could not drop my clients. A colleague heard of a new all-volunteer agency that had offices near the site of Ground Zero. But that agency presented some questionable ethical requirements that I could not accept. I withdrew my offer to help.

Two months passed without a concrete idea of how I might offer my skills in a situation of such overwhelming need. I felt dispirited by my three failed attempts. At the same time, I remembered how badly shaken I had been by my experience at Bellevue Hospital and by the whole 9/11 tragedy. I questioned whether, in the first two weeks, I could have given objective support. Now that I had gained some perspective and balance, what was I to do? I prayed for the answer.

At breakfast the next morning, *The New York Times* special section on people who had died in the tragedy of 9/11 published a profile of Stephen Hoffman, who had perished in the collapse of the first World Trade Center tower. He was an identical twin. His brother, Greg, had been interviewed, and had given a moving tribute to his beloved twin's life. I read his words as if he had spoken them in my presence. Without hesitation, I picked up the phone and called Jane Gross, the reporter who wrote the piece. After introducing myself to her as a trained psychotherapist, I told her I had lost my twin.

"I would be very grateful," I said, "if you'd be willing to contact the family and give them the message that if they need a therapist with my background, I'd be most willing to help."

Jane passed on my message and phone number. With renewed hope, I went back to work and to wait. Two weeks later, my office phone rang, just after I'd hung up with my next scheduled client who had called in sick. The phone call was from Aileen Hoffman, the wife of Gregory Hoffman, Stephen Hoffman's twin.

"Do you have time to talk?" she asked.

With inner excitement, I replied, "I do."

Aileen explained that her husband was deeply upset and depressed—unable to go to work. He had refused to go back to the psychotherapist she'd called in after his twin's death, saying the therapist did not understand how he felt. We spent forty minutes on the phone. I found out she was also a clinical social worker specializing in trauma therapy at a large agency in Long Island. She asked questions about my training, my perspective on twin loss, and whether I had healed from my own personal loss. At the end of our conversation, she asked if I would be willing to do bereavement counseling with her husband.

"Why don't we see if he'd be willing to come in," I answered. "Then he and I can judge together whether we'd be a good fit."

Greg and I met and agreed to begin working together. I was struck by the strength of his religious faith, which lay beneath his despair, and identified with his enormous pride in his twin. At home, while he struggled with his loss, Greg and his wife looked for others whose twins had died on September 11, twins who might be comforted by meeting other twinless twins. About three weeks later, Aileen called with the news that they had found eleven other surviving twins in the Tristate area around New York City. (A total of forty-six twins died in the entire 9/11 disaster.) She asked if I would be interested in leading a group.

"Definitely," I replied.

With a grant from her agency, I started a 9/11 twin bereavement group in May 2002. We met once a week for two years. At our first gathering, the twins sat in a circle with me and began to share their stories. They immediately trusted one another. It was as if their twinship bound them together and allowed them to safely open their hearts. Listening to them speak, I was overcome by a fervent desire to join them, to share my story, to become a member of this group, not their leader. I remembered the gift of my own healing and my vision, which was unfolding now in front of me. Taking in my gift, I let my desire go.

The twins did beautiful work. They understood and supported each other. They shared not only the many positive memories of their twinship, but also their deep experiences of pain and disappointment and their feelings of anger, regret, and guilt, all natural parts of the grieving process. Bonded by their twinship, they found they could momentarily step out of their pain to share delightful memories with laughter. The feelings of extreme loneliness coming from their loss and the misunderstandings of family and friends were appreciated, understood, and assuaged in our group. I remembered the times when I felt misunderstood, especially by Dr. Simmons. It gave me enormous pleasure to recognize and identify with these twins' feelings and to be able to prevent any need for them to deny their reality. The power of their interconnection precluded the isolation that marked my own experience of loss. But as with the loss of Michael, most would have no physical closure. The bodies of their twins were never found.

At the end of our first year of work, I introduced them to Dr. Gallegos's spontaneous interactive imagery process. The deceased twins of some of the group members appeared in their imagery as healing guides. Within each journey and, without exception, all these twin guides expressed their well-being to their living twin, and emphasized the importance of the living twin being able to embrace his or her own individual life. With or without the healing guidance of their deceased twin, all the group participants came away from their imagery journeys with hope and with a sense of the enduring love of their twins.

After one evening meeting, two members of the group told me about their experiences after joining a large network of bereaved twins called the Twinless Twins Support Group International, or TTSGI, and they shared their enthusiasm for the five-day conference held each summer. The organization had recently lost its founder, his death bringing great sadness, as well as the group's disappointment over not being able to find a professional speaker who understood the unique issues of twin bereavement. My twins asked if I would be willing to be introduced to TTSGI and possibly be its next speaker. I sensed a door opening.

I have been to every TTSGI conference since my first invitation to speak in 2003, sometimes talking to large groups and always meeting twins in smaller counseling sessions or one-on-one. Like the TTSGI group members, those on the board of directors have each lost a twin, and with the exception of the executive director, all are volunteers.

At my first conference I was generously welcomed not only as the primary speaker but, more important to me, as a twinless twin. More than ninety twins were present, many accompanied by family members, other loved ones, or a friend. Each morning, for three days, one twin after another rose, supported by a long-term member of the group, and testified to his or her twin loss. They told the stories of their twin's death. This tradition bore witness to an ending, and it marked the moment when they could begin their healing process in a new form of twin connection. The sense of group identity, mutual love and sadness was overwhelming. Throughout that week, my heart almost burst with a new acknowledgment and sense of belonging. Over the years, my devotion to this organization has grown. Through it I have met and counseled many twinless twins. My life is continually enriched by these relationships. The hard-won insights and the perspective of my long and painful healing journey feel especially worthwhile when I support bereaved twins to heal the way they began—in connection.

CHAPTER TWENTY-SEVEN

The crow says, "I will lift up Michael's spirit to the heavens when you are ready to let it go. First, however, you must walk out with Michael through the 'valley of death.'"

MY JOURNEY OF twin loss and healing is one of thousands of such hidden journeys, each unfolding in its own unique and mysterious way. All these experiences join in a common healing process, which has its own distinctive challenges. Yet I believe the journey of twin bereavement has much to teach about the process of grieving and healing the loss of any profoundly interconnected relationship.

For many twins, losing their twin feels like the literal end of their lives. It is true, in that it is the end of life as they have known it since conception. As one twin explained to me, "After Daphne died, it was as if I could not breathe. I'd never in my life thought about breathing; I just took it for granted that Daphne's and my breath were part of being alive."

In an important symbolic sense, when one twin dies, the other must begin to breathe again; the surviving twin must begin again with his or her life, starting with what truly feels like the end.

Healing from a deep personal loss is an active process that naturally unfolds from within. It evolves through experiencing and expressing in some form the varied spontaneous and emotional memories of the relationship. This process can be carried out in many different ways, such as in group sharing, in private counseling, in journaling or in letter writing, in making music, or in other forms of creative expression. Ideally, one finds a safe place to engage with a person or persons who are willing to listen, respect, and relate to all of the unique characteristics of the twin relationship and to the individual meaning of its loss.

The challenges of the healing journey are big. Closely bonded twins often see themselves in the context of another person. The subjective "I" is viewed in a framework of "we." This intrinsic perception affects how many twins see themselves as well as how they see others. It informs the meaning they ascribe to themselves in the world. When one twin dies, the "we" is broken. The surviving twins are often left feeling like half a person. They lose their grounding and have trouble negotiating their world. Their sense of themselves can be seriously challenged.

Therefore, along with engaging in an actively involved bereavement process, these twins heal by developing and supporting their individual identity. This dual process enables lone twins to meet what I feel is the biggest challenge of their bereavement. The physical or temporal experience of twinship is destroyed in death, but the bond—imprinted in the body, mind, and heart—remains, holding on to the structure and shadow of the departed physical relationship. And because of their sense of a twinned identity, bereaved twins cling to their twinned life, afraid on unconscious and/or conscious levels of their own death if they let go. They must psychologically "die to" or release this primary temporal connection. In other words, they must let go of the twin that has already left if they are to fully heal.

Because of this intrinsic attachment and the difficult challenges it presents, the healing journey from twin loss is markedly longer than are many other types of bereavement. It is accompanied by significant levels of pain, sometimes experienced physically as well as psychologically, and as my story illustrates, persistent denial can haunt the process. Finally, the bereavement journey is driven by a deep and natural imperative to heal.

I am in awe of the universal healing force within each of us. I believe it self-activates in the psyche, just as the healing process does in the body when it is physically injured. The naturally activated inner healing process from *any* major loss is painful and long. And our culture allows only a short interval of time for its completion: only a brief time out for the shock, for the denial, for the slow, deep emotional acceptance of the death, for the healing grief that accompanies the loss and the ending of a whole way of being, and for reorienting to a new way of life. As a result, many people shy away from their inner healing process when it arises, thus never completing their healing and never again experiencing the pleasure of a full engagement in their lives or of developing a new relationship to their departed loved one or twin.

I am an example of the healing imperative's irrepressible, restoring, integrating, and transmuting force. With profound sophistication and complexity, with super strength and seeming cunning, and with and without my help, this natural healing process found its way in me to completion.

This innate process began with the inner fog that arose within me in New Guinea, with the numbness and feelings of disconnection that offered protection from an unfolding trauma I was not yet able to take in. My mother then forbade its balm of natural tears, tears that sprang forth within the safety of her embrace. My tears froze. I moved back into the protective numbness and disconnection of the first stage of healing that now no longer served me. As the months and years passed, the all-consuming events surrounding marriage, home, and children created a largely engaged life that enabled my denial of Michael's death and sidelined the bereavement imperative. It took a powerful psychological crisis that imploded that afternoon in my garage, the "healing crisis" that broke down my world of self-expectation and self-protection in order to permit nature's healing imperative to resume.

In Dr. Simmons's office, it surfaced within the good work I did to find and nurture an independent sense of self. But Dr. Simmons did not understand that a tap root of my psyche sprang from my twinship. Inadvertently, he blocked an important piece of my healing by not recognizing the personal significance of my twinship and the extended timetable of twin bereavement. But I felt this miraculous process reemerge while in my small apartment, when I took the time to listen to who I was and to allow the seminal words to be expressed: "I am a twin."

Sadly, the cultural and therapeutic misunderstandings of the twin bond brought back and reinforced my denial of Michael's death and my twinship. This denial lasted for years and masked itself as acceptance. The healing imperative went underground and waited for opportune experiences to emerge. It also disguised itself to get a foothold in my consciousness. My relationship to Mary Margaret Goodrich became the perfect setting for its next steps.

As our friendship grew, M.M. took my hand and led me on her path. With her loving, laughing, and courageous presence, she made her dying journey safe for me. She was able to open to death in its larger context; and without realizing it, in being drawn to her path, in bearing witness to her journey, I learned from M.M. how to die. I did not understand until I was halfway through writing this book that my experience with Mary Margaret became a trial run for the life-and-death transition I needed to make for myself and Michael.

I believe the alternating pain and sense of disconnection from sensation that developed on the left side of my body was a physical manifestation of the necessary dying of the twinned part of my psyche. The flow of healing was present despite my denial, and the risk of this huge inner transition was expressed in an overwhelming sense that I would die.

I have found the healing process to be astonishingly sophisticated and complex. I realize now that even my relationship to Tom, as well as to Jeremy, involved subconscious twinning efforts, the desire to recreate the original human bond that sprang from my beginnings in the womb. I have described the extraordinary waking dream I had of Jeremy (Michael) and me as tiny beings floating together, and of how that vision, coming from the deepest recesses of my being, surfaced in the context of this intimate relationship. I believe it was that open and beautiful relationship with Jeremy that allowed me to fully experience my liberated feminine self. And that freed femininity sprang from the trusting root of my twinship. In turn, it was the Jeremy relationship that opened me to the waking dream, which brought me back to Michael and my original twin bond. The healing process was working as a multifaceted force that allowed me to grow and heal as it progressed.

The waking dream of Michael and me floating together in the womb surfaced as a conscious expression of inner knowing. I needed to feel the full power of my twinship in order to grieve its physical loss. When Jeremy and I parted, my ensuing grief tapped into the huge well of unexpressed grief for Michael, but as with the waking dream, this primal grief was at first disguised. I was not yet ready. It was not until weeks later that I realized and understood that I was with Michael in my vision. In that moment of realization, I fully appreciated and accepted the importance of my twinship to my life. That realization irreversibly opened and moved me to begin the journey of accepting and actively grieving Michael's death.

At the same time, it was made possible by the support and strength I received from having developed a clear sense of myself as an individual.

The pace of my healing rapidly increased when I was able to become a partner to the inner healing imperative. I moved to fully understand the bond of twinship by reading twins' stories, memoirs, and research, and to understand my twin beginnings by talking to my nurse Pat and to my mother. Memories of Michael began to surface, but they were too painful to handle alone. I was drawn to connect to him through a reunion with his closest friends. Fully activated, the healing process surfaced unbidden when Michael's friends left our reunion weekend. It manifested itself in a breaking-open of my psyche, a breaking through to my conscious mind of the imperative to heal and the need to find a safe place where I could meet my feelings and memories. Again, the process found its way when I just happened upon a brochure for the "Returning to Earth" vision quest experience, and was able to open to the support of my yellow Labrador, Oliver, and to the wonder of finding a magnificent healing ally in nature.

People throughout the ages have told of the inner healing that comes from spending time in nature. When I stopped and took the time to become fully conscious and aware of the natural world, my life changed. I opened to a profound beauty, which sprang from connection, from interrelationship. I thrilled to bird song and sunrise; raindrops and ferns; wind and dancing treetops; morning dew, sunlight, and spider webs; the breath of warm breeze and pine scent—each entwined sensation became a healing balm for the inner disconnection I felt. Nature's life forms spread before me, inviting me to connect with them. I was offered signs and symbols for my healing path. On my Medicine Walk, the beech leaf became a mirror in which I recognized the dying I was not quite ready to acknowledge in myself and yet needed to confront. At my power spot, the bubbling rush of the stream accepted what I needed to release. It cleansed and renewed my spirit. Each night it sang me to sleep. Again and again, I discovered the alive, responsive world of nature. Nature as community banished loneliness from my solitude.

———

I AM GRATEFUL I found a place of safety and connection for my next huge steps of transition and integration during the vision quest. My inner imperative knew it was safe, knew I was ready, and pushed me into the arms of my group so I might acknowledge Michael's death and, in the same breath, release my imploding grief. From then on, it was all about opening, opening fully to the natural healing that sought to unfold. And it unfolded to completion within the imagery journeys that Steve Gallegos initially guided and that I continued on my own.

Dr. Gallegos's healing technique, described by him as "deep, personal imagery," finds within us the wisdom we constantly search for outside of ourselves. By tapping into this subconscious resource, we naturally move to integrate any experience that has overwhelmed us at the time it took place. Through inviting, dialoguing with, and being in relationship to images that spontaneously appear, the journey-er joins with his or her natural healing imperative on a path of personal and psychological integration. As I have shown, the imagery process became an all-important part of my healing, and it worked in perfect concert with the ally I had found in nature.

This spontaneous and interactive process is comprised of three traditions: the theory of "active imagination," developed by the psychological researcher and analyst Carl Jung; the Eastern medical and theoretical perspective, which understands the human being as a system of interrelated energies or chakras connected to the character of the individual psyche; and the Native American practice of speaking to and learning from animals in nature, which are revered as guides and guardians. This process is differentiated from "guided imagery," in which images are often created and/or controlled by the guide or therapist; or from hypnosis, where suggestions are made to the subconscious and, again, the journey is controlled by the therapist. It is different from imagination where our mind wanders, calling up scenes and images at will. In deep personal imagery, the images arise spontaneously from a deeper level of the subconscious that responds to the subject of the invitation, but has its own integrity and integrating, healing agenda. In Dr. Gallegos's method, the guide's or therapist's role is to help the journeyers connect and maintain their relationship to their individual inner process without controlling it. It involves a trust on the part of the guide and the journeyer in the inner healing imperative.

***

THERE IS MUCH wonder and mystery inherent in the inner workings of the psyche and in its connection to a larger framework of intelligence and power. Carl Jung talks of the synchronicity between dreams, visions, and outer manifestations. I experienced this phenomenon on the last evening of the vision quest.

On the final imagery journey of my quest, Mountain Lion brought me into the ocean on her back. There I merged with Michael, who held on to Oliver's back. On my solo and in that last profound journey, Oliver became and acted as Michael's animal of imagery—the equal partner of Mountain Lion.

That evening, after my journey and after dinner, I received a phone call from James, the caretaker of my place in the country. Oliver was staying with him and his wife while I was away. James informed me that he had taken Oliver to the veterinary hospital, suffering from water on the lungs. His condition was serious, but with treatment, the veterinarian felt he would recover. I was devastated. How could this have happened? It seemed impossible, but could my imagery have somehow affected Oliver? Was I healing at the expense of my loyal friend? I spoke with Steve Gallegos, who told me he felt, on some intrapsychic level, that Oliver had supported my healing at his own risk, and now we needed to support his. In a teepee that stood on the property a short distance from the lodge, we conducted a healing ceremony. The lodge owner's dog, Tripod, stood in for Oliver. I laid my hands on this gentle dog's chest and prayed for Oliver's healing. By the time I reached home a week later, I felt truly blessed, for when I opened the door to my house, my dear friend was there to greet me.

WITH THE LETTING go of the imprinted twin life that is no longer physically manifested, and with the reframing of the twinned identity to an individual sense of self, what is left of the twinship? This important question brings me back to a twenty-year-old woman who sat in my office. A year before, her twin sister had died in a car accident. Now this young woman had decided to reach out for help. Tears streamed down her face; her small chin stuck out trembling. She gripped the arms of her chair and ignored the Kleenex box I held out to her.

"I don't ever want to heal," she cried, "if it means I am no longer a twin."

The young woman released her grip on the chair and put her hands over her downturned face. I waited quietly. She looked up, and in barely a whisper asked, "Are *you* still a twin?"

I took the huge question in.

"Yes, I am," I replied. "When I was able to acknowledge the death of my twin brother and allow myself to grieve, I found I did not lose my twinship as I thought I would. In healing from my loss, I did not abandon my twin. I made a new kind of relationship to him. Like you,

I will always remain a twin." Very slowly, this young woman began to trust enough in me and in her own strength and safety to allow herself to open to this perspective and to follow her natural healing path.

———

THE TRUTH OF my abiding twinship to Michael surfaced in my small apartment after years of repression. But that truth is the root of who I am and remains alive today. As my healing continued after the vision quest, my twin bond expressed itself in special heartwarming ways. In my first year of fieldwork at Columbia University School of Social Work, I was placed at a single-room occupancy hotel, a five-floor walk-up in Harlem that had been turned into a residence for the homeless, most of whom were mentally ill. There, I joined the university's community health service team, which had a small office in the basement. As well as working with individual patients, I led a therapeutic women's group that met once a week. These ten women came from different races and backgrounds. Their histories were all sad, all deprived—some tragic. They had different levels of mental illness and disability. Three were schizophrenic, three alcoholic, two bipolar, one blind with a personality disorder, and one a down-and-out old lady who had lost her memory in an accident. My group was very reluctant to talk about their personal lives, so I created a thematic process for our meetings. I would read stories and diaries of women who were trying to overcome great difficulties in their lives and we would discuss them. After a time, our group began to share some of their own troubles and their own ways of dealing with them. They touched me with their pain, their courage, their creative perseverance, and their depression, which sometimes freed itself as anger. They delighted me with their outrageous humor. I felt we needed to do something to commemorate our work together, and to mark the end of the year. Unanimously, the group voted to go on an outing. After much

WHEN GRIEF CALLS FORTH THE HEALING

discussion and dissension, it was decided we would go to the New York Botanical Gardens in the Bronx, for lunch. Our agency had no money for outings. I pretended we had a special "outings grant," and put up the money myself. I asked my supervisor's permission for our group to go. She shook her head, "Mary, you're nuts." After two days of persistent appeals, she relented. I could go with the group if I assumed all of the responsibility. She would report me to the Columbia University School of Social Work if something went wrong.

God help me! I thought on my way home from work. *What have I done? How am I ever going to take ten mentally ill and disabled ladies to the Botanical Gardens for the day?* I had no idea how to get there from Harlem, especially by subway and bus. *What if Julia or Terry has a psychotic episode? What if Delia starts drinking or someone wanders off? What if we all get lost?* My worries continued to multiply. I felt out of breath. Then something odd and miraculous happened. I saw an image of Michael. He had a delighted look on his face. I could see he felt the plan was magnificent. *With everyone pulling together—of course it would work!* Fears evaporated as my excitement built. Right then I decided to include our group in the challenge.

At our next meeting I told them we had to prove to the agency that we could work together, find our way, and take care of each other. The ladies caught on. It was us against them! We looked at the tasks involved. They volunteered. A couple of women offered to find out how to get to the Botanical Gardens and back. Having been homeless, these women were inventive. Anne said she would be in charge of helping Sarah, who was blind. Someone else volunteered to be in charge of the time, and Geraldine, who once worked in an insurance agency, asked if she could use our office computer to look up the restaurants and the flower shows at the Botanical Garden. I voiced a concern: with such a big group and so many exciting things to see, it would be easy for someone to wander off and get lost. What could we do about that? Muriel, the biggest, most imposing and outspoken member of our group, stood up. She had bipolar disorder, and despite her medication, I was concerned she might be entering the early stages of the manic phase of her illness. I had some misgivings about her coming on the trip. But I knew she would be devastated if I left her behind. Now she was brimming with frenetic energy and goal-oriented plans. "I'll be in charge of keeping the group together," she announced, "keeping order, reading the menus at the restaurant, and finding the restroom—you know how important *that* is!" Everyone laughed. She raised her voice, "Most important of all, I'll be in charge of reminding everyone not to pick the flowers! I have read that you are not allowed to do that." She looked pointedly at Cynthia, the old lady who had lost her memory. Cynthia bowed her gray head. "Oh," she sighed, "I wanted so much to pick real flowers for my room." "Perhaps our grant will be big enough for us to buy postcards," I interjected. "I've seen beautiful postcards of flowers that friends of mine brought back from the gardens." Cynthia nodded sadly. Everyone added disappointed remarks. Sarah, the blind woman, stated in a cross voice that it wasn't her problem. She thought for a moment. Did I think she could touch the flowers?

Sarah did! A tall, bespectacled man in charge of the Botanical Gardens' disabilities services guided her hands gently over leaves and flower petals in the vast greenhouses that we visited on our trip. Little, angry, troubled Sarah stood smiling and mesmerized before the flowers and shrubs she connected with. Everyone felt the joy of her discovery. It seemed to enhance our own sensual pleasure in the riotous color and scents surrounding us.

Our outing was a huge success. From the two buses and subway rides we took to the cafeteria we chose for lunch; from finding the ladies' rooms to negotiating the walks and the tulip show with our maps—in all these experiences I felt the strength and connection of us as a group. All the volunteers carried out their jobs. Even Muriel calmed down, softened her aggressive, bossy tone and did her reminding with a sense of humor.

This time, on my way home from work, a rush of happiness flooded me. It swept into every memory of the day. As a group we had claimed our experience. Through Sarah we made intimate connection to the individual plants. The passionate, unrestrained blooms of the tropical flowers had touched our places of wildness and wonder. The bold, controlled patterns of color in the tulip beds had offered the boundaries we needed for our lives and our group. In the middle of the city we had made our own connection with nature. Those moments erased the color-less outer world that separated us from ourselves and from one another. Gratefully, I thought of Michael, who was never caught by these separating forces. I felt his twinship and his presence as I realized a prayer from my wilderness solo had been answered. I had taken in and expressed Mike's ability to joyfully embrace life without hesitation and fear. Michael was alive, in me.

HEALING FROM MY twin loss has not meant "moving on" as Dr. Simmons had wanted. It has meant moving forward—moving forward to become fully engaged in a new life that holds meaning for me as an individual. As the years have passed, I have sensed a growing freedom, almost as if I were being released from a spell. There have been both small, subtle and big changes in my perception of and response to events and people. Some of these changes have come about as delightful surprises, like my experience with my women's group at the Botanical Gardens, or the joy of having memories of my life with Michael without them dissolving into yearning and loss. Other changes have come with dogged and daring persistence, and with growing pains.

I am married again—this time for keeps. My husband, David, and I have been together twenty-three years. Despite all my resolve to the contrary, the issue of searching for another twinship snuck back into my life and into this primary relationship. As David and I grew more attached and committed to each other, I became once again addictively drawn to having the intimate interdependent bond I had known as an infant and young child. This expectation and need overrode the independent and professional life I was successfully developing; it simply arose as second nature. The result was deep inner conflict and confusion. David's natural reserve and independent character made any hope of twinning impossible. But I tried to change him. With hurt feelings, real pain, and sometimes anger, I banged against a boundary that held and bounced me back into my self, into my pain, and into my own strength and resources. David's stubborn independence and reserve slowly became a gift. I knew, underneath all the misunderstanding and my unrealistic expectations, that we loved each other. *David loves me—he is not and will not be my twin.*

In little pieces and over the span of years, I have let go a lot of my root expectations. In healing from Michael's death I had to release the imprint of the already departed physical relationship I treasured. In moving forward with my life, I've had to release my imprinted idea of what an intimate relationship should be. In so doing, I opened to a new and wider perception of what intimacy means. I did this with the help of therapy, my imagery, and with David's abiding loyalty and kindness, and his naturally optimistic nature. Slowly, and sometimes with a sense of great risk of abandonment, I developed the trust that we could each lead our individual lives and not lose our love and our relationship. I have learned to support and take pleasure both in David's independent interests and in mine. Our relationship is enriched and made more intimate by sharing our separate experiences and by feeling pride in each other's endeavors. And as I released the pressure on him to become my twin, David has spontaneously come forward to share more of himself.

Working with and becoming friends with other twinless twins has greatly warmed my heart and nourished my continued personal growth. Seeing them dealing with many of the same issues that I have had to face helps me appreciate the reality of my own struggle and takes away the loneliness of my inner path, through the shared gift of healthy twin connection. It has been important for me to develop my own sense of humor, patience, and self-acceptance. The rhythms of primary twinship, like musical themes, get replayed. And even when they are understood and dropped from the score, their expectant notes seem to echo. They sound in friendships as well as in love relationships. When I hear the siren notes, I catch myself. Now I can breathe in and release with a knowing inner smile. My loved ones and friends don't speak that musical language. I try to save it for the songs of the twin conferences.

———

FINALLY, AS I moved forward creating a larger, fuller, and happier context for my life, I hit an unexpected emotional roadblock, which threw me back into the raw feelings of early unintegrated loss. I knew that one of the hardest parts of any healing journey from an important loss is that it does not have a clear finish line that one can cross. I also knew that, years later, the bereaved survivor can encounter acute pain connected with the departed loved one, which finally surfaces to be healed. These deeply embedded feelings are usually not accessible until one has formed the foundation of a new life from which to draw strength. With this knowledge, I was still not ready to confront a new form of guilt and shame that had been buried for more than forty years after Michael's disappearance.

Guilt had plagued my healing journey. I had worked through "survivor's guilt" and the guilt of whether I could have done something more to prevent Michael's death. This new guilt lay deeper, and was wrapped around the grim reality of the unknown moments before Michael's death.

When I discovered the transcript of René Wassing's meeting with the press in New Guinea among Father's papers, I had to face the details of Michael's last moments on the boat and take in the known facts of his disappearance with a stark new vision. This happened more than fifteen years after I went on the vision quest. Slowly, as I unfurled my loss within this memoir, the embedded guilt found its way toward my consciousness, and two years ago, just before the annual twin conference, it surfaced. In being present in my mind and heart for Michael's last moments on the boat, my deeper feelings were freed. And I was able to face the different scenarios of what Michael could have encountered before he died.

My life began next to Michael. In the womb, our lives were intertwined. In his dying and in his death, I was not next to Michael. I had abandoned my twin by not being there with him or for him.

This deep feeling festered in my heart. It was as real and pervasive as it was irrational and self-wounding. And worse, I knew that Michael would not sanction or condone it. From my past experience, I knew that a key part of releasing guilt is meeting and expressing its reality. At the twin conference, as I have described, each twin stands and tells the story of his or her twin's death and then moves forward with their healing in new twin connection. As a keynote speaker and a therapist for these twins, I had never gotten up to bear witness to my own loss. It was assumed by all, myself included, that I had, essentially, completed my healing. In this sense I was the twins' example, their hope, the Sherpa on their path. And, in that context, getting up to bear witness felt impossible.

On the second day of the 2010 twin conference, I found myself sitting close to the front of the conference room. As I listened to the twins, I began to feel distracted and distanced from the stories of their loss. I could not take in the words of the last twin's testimony. My own feelings of having abandoned Michael surfaced and merged with the anguished tone of the twin's voice. Anguish rose in my throat. A force began to move me, over which I had no control. Dazed, I got up as the young woman sat down. I told Michelle, the director, I needed to speak not as a leader, but as a twin. She looked at me and understood. She told the group there was one more testimony. Dave, the veteran guardian and supporter of each twin speaker, rose to stand beside me.

The other twins fully understood the current of distress that poured from my heart. They held me in loving silence as I released my guilt and my shame. When I finished, one by one, they came up to touch me or give me a hug. One twin said, "We knew you were there for us, there to help us; but now you have truly become one of us." The others nodded.

———

"HAVE YOU EVER asked yourself where Michael is now?"

My close friend, Eileen, and I were talking about our twins and my writing this book, which was nearing completion, when she asked this mysterious question. She had been pondering it in relationship to her own twin sister. Since fully releasing the sense of having abandoned Michael, I was feeling particularly close to him. Now I experienced her question as if it were a door waiting to be opened. I told her I needed to find a quiet spot and listen for the answer.

———

Back at home, I went to a secluded place where I sat beneath trees and against a rock, about two feet from a stream. The place reminded me of my solo, of my "power spot" on my vision quest.

I settled my body against the support of the rock and thought of the long twisted path of my healing and of my last imagery journey on the vision quest, where the crow lifted homeward that piece of Michael that I had held back.

"Where are you now, Mike?" I asked.

Awareness of dappled sun and stirring leaves joins this question. My eyes close; the air glides through my nostrils, drawing my attention inward.

Breathing in—breathing out . . .

Quieting . . . letting go . . .

Now I breathe in a breath of knowing—a breath of knowing so deep, so wide, it is bigger than the air. It fills my awareness with a vision.

I feel you here with me, Mike. I know you.

You are in the places of beauty and meaning, which you followed your whole life; the sacred harmony you recognized in New Guinea and sought to cherish and reveal.

I know it now. You had already died when I arrived. You were there that afternoon in Amanamkai. You came to me on the pier. I saw through your eyes the synchronized rowers in that canoe. I felt your excitement. I felt you in the connection between those beautiful men and their curved boat, merged with their energy that flowed through shining, rolling forms into paddles, into balancing legs and feet. I felt you in the joining of these men, their canoe, and the water.

I know you came to me, Mike—you reached out to me through the old lady's tear-filled eyes, through her ancient, gentle hands. It was you within her compassion showing me I was connected, not abandoned, not hopelessly lost, not forever alone.

Now I find you in the carved Asmat shield, in the cylindrical drum, in the huge wooden bis pole. I enter your passion. I feel you in the artist's hand as it carves a new gift from the tree. I follow you through the bis pole carving, into the moving force of its ceremony; into the pulsing sound, into the fever of powerful, shifting shapes.

Together we join the Asmat people in their death-releasing ritual, enter their naked loss and yearning. We enter in connection. There is no isolation, no loneliness. Together we listen, experience, and bear witness.

I join you in this ceremonial gift of releasing. I join your courage. With you I join the rhythm of life and death and life again.

After the ceremony, we become the towering bis pole as it is allowed to fall to the ground. Brave-faced men pick us up and carry us like a coffin to the familial woods from whence we sprang. There, they leave us, discarded, returned to the earth, allowed to rot, to fall apart—to become the mother of a new tree.

Your whole life was this discovery, Mike. In your dying, in my dying, in our dying, I found you. I feel your love, your wide, wise embrace. My vision quest allowed me to join yours. Thank you with all my heart.

Michael Rockefeller, Balim Valley, New Guinea, 1961

EPILOGUE

―――――――――――――――――――――――

"I HAVE NO sense of who I am or how to live on my own," Margaret tearfully admitted, six months after the death of her husband and the subsequent end of her forty-five-year marriage to a loving, controlling man who ran their social and financial life.

My client Molly, in losing her only child, told me that her life held no meaning. "Little Tim was everything to me; I am nothing now that I am not a mother."

Harold and Sam grew up as inseparable brothers one year apart. They shared a room and went to the same high school. They cheered each other on as members of the varsity tennis team. When Harold died in a car accident at 16, Sam dropped off the team and refused to apply to college, saying he and Sam had not decided where they wanted to go. As he spoke, Sam's voice shook with fierce despair. "Without Harold, I have no sense of what I want now," he said. "Nor do I care."

Writing this memoir has focused my awareness and increased my sensitivity to the mostly hidden trauma of death and loss and the important role it plays in all human life and love relationships. Twin loss, with its mirrored images and seminal bond, and with its challenge of developing an individual identity, magnifies and illuminates the universal experience of loss.

The severing of a love relationship through death fractures the foundation of the bereaved. Our culture's common belief that one "must rapidly get up and move on" after such a loss results in denying death and repressing grief. This societal pressure adds to the trauma, creating isolation and misunderstanding, and separates us from our natural inner healing process. But, even beyond the power and influence of our culture, we deeply fear our own grief.

When I finally allowed myself to feel the truth of Mike's death that first night on the vision quest, I was terrified I would drown in the resulting tide of tears. My friend Emily, who lost her fiancé in our invasion of Iraq, told me that she no longer reads the daily newspaper or goes to a sad movie; nor is she willing to watch a disturbing play. She is frightened she might start to weep and be overtaken by her grief. Emily lives a life of anxiety and exaggerated daily fears that, though seemingly unrelated to her loved one's death, express the feelings of loss she denies. She wants to find another love, but her relationships remain shallow and unfulfilling in her efforts to keep control over her emotions.

Why does experiencing our grief feel so life-threatening? I believe we subconsciously fear that if we truly grieve our loved one's death, we will also die. Beyond the seminal dread that twins feel, which comes from the death of a paired twin identity, all people who have deeply bonded with another person lose in death—in the shattering of that physical connection—an important part of themselves. In that sense, a part of us does die. In grieving, we allow ourselves to open to that double loss. In grieving, we are acknowledging the death of what no longer exists.

"It is so important to tell people," my old friend from San Diego said over lunch. "We are clueless about grieving and death. After my son Jason died, I was lost to myself. I became agitated and so afraid of what lay deep inside. I was pushing forward with a life that couldn't be open and that couldn't listen. I had no idea that my body knew the healing path if I could but stop, and trust, and dare to let go."

One of the ironies of human existence is that it is our grieving that calls forth our healing. And, like the journeyers out of twin loss, we all, in having the courage to feel and express the emotional memories of our relationship, are honoring and witnessing our loved ones' lives.

Each slow, painful step allows the transformation of a relationship that can no longer be present for us in physical form. Each step allows us to support the formation of a new sense of self. Each step also brings us closer to re-experiencing our cherished memories, the gift of our beloved, and our mutual love without crippling pain. And by our trust and willingness to allow the ending, we are opening ourselves and our lives to a new beginning.

ACKNOWLEDGMENTS

DURING THE SIX years it took me to write this book and bring it to publication, I've experienced countless acts of kindness, emotional support, and professional assistance. To all those who helped, each in their special way, I offer my deepest gratitude—in particular, I want to thank:

Marcy Vaughn, my colleague and close friend, whose wisdom and steadfast dedication to my process made it possible for me to reenter the dark place of loss in safety and to retrace the steps of my healing process. She guided the imagery journeys I took along the way, transcribed my handwritten manuscript, worked with me cutting and editing, and most important, helped me in difficult places to listen for what held truth and meaning.

Joe Pittman, my editor, for his quiet and important endorsement of my writing and the creative integrity of my memoir, for his clear, beneficial, editorial suggestions, and for his advocacy.

Amy Hertz of Tangerine Ink, my publishing consultant, for her enthusiasm and sensitivity, for her amazing publishing experience, and for her acute listening skills and talent, which led to perfect timing and excellent editorial support. And to Marc Haeringer, her assistant, for all the important and organizational help and details I am not even aware of.

Laura Carton, my highly valued assistant, for her many creative and skilled technological services and organizational assistance—for her wide experience, loyalty, perseverance and expertise, and for the laughter and hard work we share together.

I am grateful to all the readers of my memoir, whose thoughtful, helpful advice and heartfelt support have been invaluable. I especially want to thank Victoria Menzies, Betsy Griffith, Eileen Growald, Kathy Benners, my sister-in-law Barbara Rockefeller, Susan Gillotti, and Janet Lowenthal; also, Sam Roberts, Peter Johnson, Nancy Geary, Judith Goldstein, Mel Bucholtz, and Steve Gallegos.

During the writing process, I became particularly indebted to Barbara Trimble, Rachel Naomi Remen, Jo Ann Miller, Robert Oxnam, Trebbe Johnson, and Andrew Kimbrell for the precious gift of their wisdom, experience, and focused advice, all of which have immeasurably affected and benefitted my book.

I have been gifted by the moral support, enthusiasm and encouragement from my twin pals Michelle Getchell and Dena Stitt, and from my sister-in-law Sascha Rockefeller; also from Marie Salerno, Margaret Vasington, Alicia Sainer, and the Woodstock Imagery Group. I offer special thanks to my oldest friend, Betsy Gotbaum, for her loyal support and generosity.

I give thanks to Tomasa Arevalo, Blanca Medina, Elba Benegas, Ana Maria Espinosa, and Ricardo Wong for their consistent thoughtfulness, loyalty, and wonderful care.

WHEN GRIEF CALLS FORTH THE HEALING

I extend additional thanks to all of the good people who supported the publication and marketing of the hardcover and paperback edition, with very special gratitude to Joan Feeney.

Any self-doubts and discouragement I experienced during the six-year writing and publishing process was miraculously disarmed and dismissed by the ebullient enthusiasm, confidence, and encouragement of Louise Hartwell and Barbara Trimble. I will always be grateful to these dear friends.

My family is my precious foundation. I give special thanks for the thoughtful and important support of my children, Michael, Geoffrey, and Sabrina, and gratitude to my sister, Ann, for her confidence and faith in my book. I'm particularly thankful to my brother Steven for his loving acknowledgment, for his positive, thoughtful reactions to my memoir, and for the subsequent healing and blossoming of our relationship.

Finally, I offer my deepest gratitude to my husband, David, for his listening; for his calm, consistent care and patience throughout my long, challenging journey; for his carefully considered and good judgments; for his many readings and the final essential copyedit of my manuscript; and most important to me, for his belief that my experience could hold value for others. At the end of it all, I will be forever grateful for his loving me and for allowing me to experience intimacy outside of my twinship.

ABOUT THE AUTHOR

Mary Rockefeller Morgan, LMSW, is a licensed psychotherapist and certified imagery guide and trainer. She has had a general psychotherapy practice in Manhattan since 1991 and is now specializing in twin loss and bereavement counseling.

Receive more information or share your thoughts on
When Grief Calls Forth the Healing in the following ways:

www.whengriefcallsforththehealing.com

whengriefcallsforththehealing@gmail.com

Or write to:
When Grief Calls Forth the Healing
P.O. Box 219
Cross River, NY 10518-0219

OPEN ROAD

INTEGRATED MEDIA

Open Road Integrated Media is a digital publisher and multimedia content company. Open Road creates connections between authors and their audiences by marketing its ebooks through a new proprietary online platform, which uses premium video content and social media.

Made in the USA
Lexington, KY
08 May 2014